SHARING THE GOSPEL

GOOD NEWS ON THE GO

Practical Evangelism

Matthew A. Davis, DTL
Marchelle D. Lee, Th.D.

ISBN 979-8-88644-283-0 (Paperback)
ISBN 979-8-88644-285-4 (Hardcover)
ISBN 979-8-88644-284-7 (Digital)

Covenant Books
11661 Hwy 707
Murrells Inlet, SC 29576
www.covenantbooks.com

Sharing the Gospel
Good News on the Go
Practical Evangelism

Lead Authors
Matthew A. Davis and Marchelle D. Lee

Contributing Authors
Brian Bakke, Richard Booker, Sharon Booker, Carolyn J. Davis,
Allen Grimes, Sally Hinzie, Jeff Jackson, L. Paulette Jordan,
Pam Lilly, Ayanna A. Lynn, Bryan McCabe, Mike Mercurio,
Arletha Orr, Richard J. Rose, Lawrence Scott, Wille A. Taylor,
Stephen C. White, and Herron Wilson

Editors
Theresa L. Miller, Lead Editor
Cora Bigwood, Meg Bunting and Jeramie J. Salters, Editors

DEDICATION

I dedicate this book to all those who have trained me in effective Evangelism. This list is too exhaustive to include everyone. However, I give praise to the late Pastor and Superintendent Burton Clemons, his wife Gene, Assistant Pastor Terrance Curtain and wife Linda, the late Superintendent Robert and wife Emma Burel, the late Bishop Mark Conley, his wife Cynthia, Bishop Destry C. Bell Sr., and Reatha Bell, and my mentor of many years, Pastor Leo Franklin. Thank all of you for the many lessons learned and the opportunities granted. Additionally, I dedicate this book to all the pastors and ministries that opened their doors to help me develop my evangelistic gift and the souls that responded by accepting the Lord Jesus Christ into their lives.

Furthermore, I give accolades and praise to God for Mother Jewel Kirkland, who won me to Jesus Christ at a cabaret party who displayed a different lifestyle to me. Above all, I dedicate this book to every person in every nation who reads and exercises its Kingdom approach principles to introduce others to Jesus Christ as Lord and Savior of all people! Thus, souls are saved all over the world!

—Dr. Marchelle D. Lee

CONTENTS

FOREWORD

Simple but profound! Practical but inspiring! Real life but compelling! Authors Matthew Davis and Marchelle Lee have done an excellent job creating the need for evangelism, the practical ways churches, schools, and organizations can engage in soul winning and the heartfelt examples of success stories. The Church that Jesus established during His earthly ministry has lost focus of her purpose, faithfulness of the people, the force to lead, and even her future is questionable. During this critical season, it's imperative that the Church equip our members to be soul winners who have a heart for evangelism and discipleship. How do we win souls and grow saints?

The authors not only give us the ingredients for success (love, hope, and God's Word), but they also give us a practical system for enhancing or implementing an evangelistic heartbeat. Using the analogy of understood positions such as interns, paramedics, nurses, therapists, and pharmacists, they walk the readers through to prepare, pinpoint, personalize, picturize, and prescribe. Finally, they offer us real examples of lives changed, strategies implemented, and just the overall success of churches and individuals that simply got intentional in soul winning.

—Dr. Bartholomew Orr
Senior Pastor of Brown Missionary Baptist Church
Southaven, Mississippi

THE MURMURS
A Call to Action

I am grateful for the opportunity to read the powerful book written by Dr. Matthew A. Davis and Dr. Marchelle D. Lee with contributions from other pastors, ministers, and leaders. After reading the testimony of Dr. Davis's healing, I am inspired to share what I learned and how the testimony enlightened me.

Our heart murmurs are our call to action. The murmurs alert us to our need for growth. The murmurs of our heart sound out the need for us to converge toward becoming more like Jesus Christ. Our murmurs may be difficult to locate, but they are indicative that our prayers for healing must continue. We must not be alarmed by the murmur or the sound, but we must make a sound of gratitude to God that reverberates and transforms our murmurs to sounds of prayer and praise for the healing, grace, and mercy given to us by our Lord and Savior, Jesus Christ.

Evangelism can be done in many ways. This book discusses the diversity in the world. It sets forth ministerial strategies to awaken others to the need to accept Jesus Christ and the way, truth, and life He gives us when we accept Him as our personal Savior. The importance of communication enriched with precepts in the Word of God helps to build connections and commonalities and thereby urge the listeners to consider a higher dimension or realm of understanding that converges to the depth and completeness that Jesus Christ provides in our lives.

Music is also a way of awakening our youth and elders. The rhythmic metrics and soothing tones in Gospel music appeal to the receptive ears of young people who respond by taking in the wisdom of the lyrics. The recursions and repetitions in music help to build retention of the wisdom embedded in the lyrics of the songs. Music, therefore, is a powerful tool of evangelism.

This book has inspired me and others to do deeper study and to pray to become prepared, positioned, and protected by the Holy Spirit as we seek ways of optimizing our efforts to evangelize men, women, boys, and girls in the culturally diverse world population. The boundaries of our work in evangelism must be extended as we obey the call of the Great Commission.

—Dr. Jacqueline Brannon-Giles
Professor at Texas Southern University
Professor at Houston Community College

My role in this book is as editor. I had been praying how God would use me and also wanted to develop a deeper relationship with Him. God brought these desires to life by bringing a new neighbor into my neighborhood, Dr. Marchelle Lee. She invited me to her Bible study, and our friendship and my desires to grow closer to God and be used by Him blossomed from there.

Dr. Lee told me she and Dr. Davis were writing a book and I offered to edit it for them. I never expected the riches I would receive from them and the various contributing writers; I definitely received more than I gave. You see, I was one of those people who knew God wanted Christians to bring unsaved people to Him, but thought that there were prerequisites such as: one had to have a lot of Bible knowledge, the ability to quote volumes of scripture, and you had to have led a very holy life. I knew that was not me, but the more I read the words as I was editing the book, I realized I could help bring people to Christ, I just had to be willing and ask God to lead me. This book is an amazing instruction book on how to win souls for Christ. The stories in the book showed me how easy it is, the only prerequisite needed was the desire to see others save, to speak, live, and show unconditional love for my fellow man.

—Tessa Miller
Lead Editor

Sharing the Gospel, Good News on the Go is just what's needed by all of us who are pastors. It is the long-awaited tool to be used in the equipping of the saints for the work of the ministry. This book grants us proven techniques to teach, reach, and preach on a long sought-after level. Although the Bible is packed with God's Word encouraging Christians to share their faith, statistics reflect that only 10 percent of us share our faith on a regular basis. Only 5 percent have ever led a person to Christ. And finally, approximately 2 percent of us have dedicated ourselves and our ministries to reach the unsaved and to help them to become fully devoted followers of Christ. Yes, this book is a precious commodity in the hands of the believer and the non-believer. It is simply amazing how it captures the readers' attention and teach principles of divine truths throughout the book. The authors Dr. Davis and Dr. Lee draw parallels of the physical heart to the spiritual heart. Medical terms are used to reveal spiritual truths. The desire to win souls and inspire others to a deeper awareness of evangelism is clearly evident in *Sharing the Gospel, Good News on the Go.* It is a valuable book that challenges the unbeliever as well as the believer. I highly recommend this book to every pastor, Bible teacher, church leader, and lay person. It will transform your church, membership, and community.

My brother in Christ, Matthew Davis, is a man after God's own heart. He is "living proof of a loving God to a watching world."

Brother Matthew not only talks the talk, but he also walks the walk.

God has allowed me to preach and to serve as a pastor for over sixty-five years, fifty-four of which were as the founding pastor of the Sagemont Church in Houston, Texas.

I was raised in the home of a pastor and have had the opportunity over the years to come alongside hundreds of pastors. Matthew Davis has always been, and still is, one of my favorite pastoral brothers.

When God called Matthew to preach, God anointed him to be a pastor, as well. Jesus "went about doing good." My brother, Matthew, is an anointed preacher of God's Word. However, when his Bible is closed and his sermon is finished, he leaves the pulpit and continues to shepherd his flock.

Pastor Matthew loves his wife, Carolyn, his children, and his church family. At the same time, he ministers to his brothers and sisters in Christ.

I believe that when Brother Matthew stands before our Lord Jesus Christ, who is King of Kings and Lord of Lords, he will not hear the words, "Well said," but rather, "Well done, my good and faithful servant."

—Dr. John Morgan
Pastor Emeritus Sagemont Church, Houston, Texas

ACKNOWLEDGMENTS

Lead Authors
Matthew A. Davis and Marchelle D. Lee

Contributing Authors
Brian Bakke, Richard Booker, Sharon Booker, Carolyn J. Davis,
Allen Grimes, Sally Hinzie, Jeff Jackson, L. Paulette Jordan,
Pam Lilly, Ayanna A. Lynn, Bryan McCabe, Mike Mercurio,
Arletha Orr, Richard J. Rose, Lawrence Scott, Wille A. Taylor,
Stephen C. White, and Herron Wilson

Editors
Theresa L. Miller, Lead Editor
Cora Bigwood, Meg Bunting and Jeramie J. Salters, Editors

MY SALVATION STORY
Matthew A. Davis

During my junior year in high school, on a warm spring day, Tuesday, May 6, 1980, at 2:30 p.m., I met Jesus the Christ. As we sat in Mrs. Barner's sixth-period geometry class, room 2, across the hall from the cafeteria, at Gentry High School in Indianola, Mississippi, Dorothy Steele, my classmate opened a life-changing conversation with me about salvation—my salvation. You see, Dorothy was the well-known Christian girl on the campus. She was a senior and had spent the last four years demonstrating her walk in Christianity. She carried herself differently than any other person. She was intelligent, pretty, and pleasant. Dorothy always stood out among all other young ladies on Gentry's campus. When Dorothy spoke, people listened. She knew just how to get one's attention. She would look, smile, and then speak. I called it the Dorothy Effect.

I was a good person growing up; life was good. Both my parents were living. I had a stable upbringing. I never went without the necessities of life. I treated people right. I respected my elders. I set a good example for my younger siblings. I was a good boy. My friends considered me good. I was always the designated driver. I even attended church regularly, on my own accord. To me, I was in good shape. I thought that nothing was missing.

Then it happened. Unannounced, Dorothy Steele turned around, looked into my eyes, and said, "You do not have to continue living the way you are. You can be changed right here, in this room, right now. You can know for sure that you are going to heaven. You do not have to wonder about it. You can be born again, right now. You do not need a church building, a piano, or a preacher. Birds do not have to sing or fly around the room. The sky does not have to open. The earth does not have to quake. But you must repentantly believe that Jesus Christ is the Son of God who gave His life as a ransom for you and me." She continued by saying: "According to John 3:16 and Romans 10:9–10, you will be saved if you believe (trust) the gospel story of Jesus Christ. You must believe that Jesus died, was buried, and rose from the dead. The Bible teaches that if you trust in this simple story, you will be saved and go to heaven when you die. 1 Corinthians 15:1–5 presents us with the very basis of salvation. Here you will find the gospel message as described by the Apostle Paul. Paul explains that there are four pillars of the gospel: Jesus's death, Jesus's burial, Jesus's resurrection, and Jesus's appearance (evidence). Can you believe according to Romans 5:8 that over two thousand years ago, Jesus gave His life for you before you were born? You are not too bad or too far away from God for Him to save you. God will save your soul if you allow Him. Please trust Him and Him alone."

I bowed my head that day and invited Jesus into my life as my personal savior. Hallelujah, I was saved from the penalty of sin, the power of sin, and the future presence of sin! I am on my way to heaven! I will spend eternity with Jesus!

After that, I continued studying God's word and hearing His word in order to grow spiritually strong. Through studying God's word, my trust and convictions in the God of my salvation have been fortified. I believe in the Holy Trinity, which is God in three persons: God the Father, God the Son (Jesus), and God the Holy Spirit. I believe this Triune God is the only true and only living God. Any other thing, person, or substance worshipped is an idol and false God. God the Father is our creator as seen in Genesis chapter 1. Therein, Trinity is also supported, "Let us." God created everything and there is nothing that exists without the creation of the Almighty God, our Father. Jesus is God's only "begotten," unique sinless Son who gave His life for sin and sinners (John 1). He is our Savior and desires to be our Lord. As savior, He has delivered us who received Him from the destruction and damnation of hell. He is the only one qualified to redeem us from our sins. He made it possible on Calvary's Hill when he died for us. Jesus is the visible image of the invisible God. Jesus is God. He is the second person of the Triune God. The Holy Spirit is the third person of the Trinity (1 John 5:7). He is the one who dwells in every believer upon receiving Jesus Christ as Savior. The Holy Spirit keeps us sealed until the day of redemption (Ephesians 4:30). He, the Holy Spirit, gives us strength to survive in the world and in this world's system. The Holy Spirit is God. I am amazed and appreciative that the Awesome God has chosen to live in me.

I believe the Holy Bible is God's word to all humanity. The Bible is every Christian's handbook for life. The Bible gives evidence, stories, and examples of God's grace, mercy, and wrath. It gives us guidance and commandments that as we follow them, God blesses us. If we choose to disobey God's word, we become separated from God and His blessings.

THE AUTHOR'S HEART

On September 5, 1995, at eight o'clock in the morning, God pricked my heart for this ministry. I was rolled into Southwest Memorial Hospital to be prepped for open-heart surgery. The doctor proceeded to perform a heart catheterization that revealed a change in my heart condition that was different from his observation on May 17, 1995. In just four short months, my condition changed drastically! While lying on the table in the operating room, Dr. W. Carter Grinstead pronounced he saw no need for surgery at this time or in the future. He cancelled the open-heart surgery.

After I was taken to the recovery room, I asked Dr. Grinstead in amazement, "To what do *you* contribute the cancellation of my surgery?"

He replied, "Over a period of time, it (my heart) healed itself."

However, I boldly replied, "A condition that had existed for thirty-two years could not have simply healed itself in four months." I then asked, "Doctor, would you say that there was some divine intervention?"

His reply was, "No!"

Then I said, "I'm glad you used the word 'healed' because I know that man can treat, but only God can heal."

Since that day, Turning Hearts Ministries (THM) has been "Turning Hearts toward God!"

As founder and president, I am truly grateful to God for all that He has done through THM. I am deeply humbled by and appreciative of every board member, volunteer, student, pastor, benefactor, and contributor. They play key roles in our lifetime commitment to winning souls and establishing Christian-based community outreach programs. I ascribe my vision and success to their relentless commitment and support to THM.

I am overwhelmingly moved and motivated by the prayers, participation, and services of those who answered the call to be soul winners for Christ Jesus (Matthew 28:18–20). Your decision to lift up the name of Jesus says much concerning your personal Christian convictions. It says that not only are you followers of our Lord and Savior, Jesus *the* Christ, but also that your hearts burn for others to know Him as well! It is, therefore, my fervent prayer that through the studying of this book, you feel empowered to do even greater works to glorify the Savior, replenish the saints, and convert sinners. May you continue to strive for Christian excellence and never dwell in mediocrity! "He that winneth souls is wise" (Proverbs 11:30b).

SHARING THE GOSPEL, GOOD NEWS ON THE GO

The authors' intent of this book is that you will be assured of your own salvation and learn effective soul winning through practical evangelism. These techniques are biblically sound and supported by the scriptures.

Curriculum Overview

Focus: To keep Jesus Christ the main attraction, the key subject, and the center of attention (John 12:32)

Purpose: To instruct and equip you in effective soul winning (2 Timothy 2:15)

Theme: To share the Gospel of Jesus Christ unto salvation (2 Corinthians 5:17)

Goal: To equip you (the soul winner) with effective faith-based tools in acclaiming Jesus as the Christ (Matthew 28:18–20)

Method: To study, learn, memorize, and obey God's Word (2 Timothy 2:15)

Key Concept: To believe unto righteousness and confess unto salvation (Romans 10:9–10)

Resource: The Holy Bible

Supporting References: Bible Concordance, Bible Dictionary, Webster's Dictionary, and Tracts

Recommended Readings: *Eternal Security* by Charles Stanley and *Peace with God* by Billy Graham

Required Materials: Notepad, Sharing the Gospel book, and the Holy Bible. Journaling and notetaking are strongly advised while reading this book.

INTRODUCTION
Melissa

This is Melissa! She is young, beautiful, and vibrant. She looks as if she really has it all together. She does not have broken bones, bruises, scratches, and marks on her body nor does she have any mental disorders. It appears that Melissa is perfect! However, that is simply not the case. Melissa has a problem! She has a serious heart condition and will need a heart transplant! Melissa will die if she doesn't receive immediate attention from the doctor. Please understand that her heart condition is not physical, but of a spiritual nature. Melissa is no different from any one of us. As a matter of fact, she is identical to all of us. We all suffer from this same problem. We had no choice in the matter. We were born with this condition, passed down from Adam and Eve. It is sin! She is just like you are or once were! She is guilty and sentenced to die! In essence, Melissa will die unless we can help her. We must get her to the Doctor.

In order to be successful in helping Melissa, you must consider her your child. When it's your child, it becomes personal. When it's your child, it becomes an emergency. When it's your child, you try everything possible to save her life. When it's your child, you do whatever it takes to get your child to the Doctor. You must understand that neither you nor I will ever be the Doctor. We are interns, nurses, and technicians that refer patients to the doctor. It is an emergency, and we are responsible for getting the patient to the Doctor—the Great Physician—Jesus the Christ.

"Turning Hearts toward God" is not merely an engaging slogan at Turning Hearts Ministries (THM), it is our mission. THM shapes the body of Christ by advocating strong soul winning programs in families, ministries, study groups, and churches throughout the community.

We believe that when a person's heart is turned toward God, he or she becomes a new creature in Christ. The individual is no longer the same, but new. Paul writes concerning this new nature, "Therefore if any man be in Christ, he is a new creature: old things are passed away, behold, all things become new" (2 Corinthians 5:17).

The authors pray that *Sharing the Gospel, Good News on the Go* will be an effective soul winning tool. Our prayer is that those who read and study this book will gain spiritual insight into the witnessing experience. Witnessing must not be an option for the Christian. Rather, we should be compelled to win others to Christ in obedience to Matthew 28:18–20. Therefore, we should witness because: (1) God commands us, (2) there should be a great desire to assist others in going to heaven, (3) we sharpen our skills the more often we witness, and (4) Christians gain lasting joy from watching God change lives.

Remember, one must be governed by certain Christian standards of conduct during any soul winning encounter. These three essentials: Love, Hope, and God's Word are crucial elements of your soul winning presentation.

- *Love*. Exemplify the love of Christ in all that you say and do. God's love fills your life and gives you the ability to reach out to others (1 Corinthians 13:13).
- *Hope*. Undergird yourself with faith and hope. Commission the ministering spirits to go forth in providing hope to others. Their hope will grow as they realize that they can be delivered from their past by Christ's death and resurrection (Romans 5:2–5).

- *God's Word.* Feast on God's Word by studying the Holy Scriptures daily. Point to Christ and not to yourself (1 Thessalonians 2:6–8). Equip yourself to support the salvation story through the Word of God by committing key passages of scripture to memory. It is your privilege and responsibility to read, study, understand, and rightly divide God's Word when telling it to others (2 Timothy 2:15).

Main scriptures:
2 Chronicles 16:9 • Acts 1:8

Key soul winning scriptures:
1 Corinthians 15:1–5 • Matthew 28:19–20
John 3:16–17 • Acts 2:21; 4:12
Romans 3:23; 6:23; 5:8; 8:1; 10:9–10, 13, 17; 12:1–2
Ephesians 2:8–9
1 Peter 2:9 • Acts 16:31; 8:37–39; Acts 13:47 • Psalms 51
Luke 19:10

The situation is critical!
The message is urgent!
We are called to witness!

PASTORAL EVANGELISM
Lawrence Scott

The Apostle Paul, in the final year of his life, shortly before his execution, shares with Timothy his son in the ministry, four timeless imperatives, "But you, be sober in all things, endure hardship, do the work of an evangelist, fulfill your ministry" (2 Timothy 4:5). It is the work of an evangelist that is in focus here. Here, Timothy is reminded that as part of his pastoral responsibility, he should be willing and ready to announce the good news, to preach the gospel. Preaching the gospel is not only the responsibility of young Timothy, but this apostolic imperative is also a command for any person called to the pastoral ministry. We bear the responsibility of urging people to trust Jesus alone for salvation.

PREACHING JESUS

First, pastors must preach the gospel. It is vital that pastors are clear, compelling, and decisive when it comes to a frequent proclamation of Jesus as savior. The Gospel Message should be central in our preaching with the goal of people responding by faith. I marvel at God's choosing of those to the pastorate and the diversity of styles presented across pulpits on Sunday mornings. Whereas some use props to convey the message, some use tattered Bibles with torn pages to preach the timeless truth. Whether topical preaching, expository preaching, clever sermon series, or line by line teaching, our preaching should urge people to place their faith in Jesus. We must convey grace and conviction, God's mercy and repentance. When we fail to make the gospel central in our preaching, we abandon the work as evangelists. Do not abandon the work!

EVANGELISTIC PRAYERS

Second, pray evangelistic prayers. Every time the saints gather in corporate worship, we often take advantage of the moments after the sermon to pray specifically for the lost. We recognize that God saves, and He uses his people as instruments to reach others. How humbling it is to see people respond in faith in these moments. Praying during the worship service should be one of many places where we are specifically praying for the lost. As leaders in the local church, how often do we pray evangelistic prayers for those in our family? I have a family member that has rejected Christ so often that I neglected to keep him in my prayers. How often do you pray for your lost neighbor? Do we lead our church to pray for the lost in other countries or only focus on what is before us? Do we call missionaries by name and their reach into remote areas? The point is that we must do the work of an evangelist, and that work includes how we pray.

EQUIPPING THE SAINTS

Third, we must equip the saints to be evangelistic. As Paul taught, "And He gave some *as* apostles, and some *as* prophets, and some *as* evangelists, and some *as* pastors and teachers, for the equipping of the saints for the work of service, to the building up of the body of Christ" (Ephesians 4:11–12). What is evident is that all the saints and not just a few leaders are involved in the work of the ministry. Evangelism is a part of the work of the ministry. As some may be specially gifted in evangelism, all believers are responsible for following the Great Commission and making disciples (Matt. 28:18–20). If you consider the expansion of the early church, it not only included the leadership of people like Peter and Paul, but also scripture reminds us that "Those who had been scattered went about preaching the word" (Acts 8:4). They were proclaiming the gospel to those they encountered, and the Lord added to the church. Equipping the saints to be evangelistic is the work of an evangelist. As pastors, are we training the members to be evangelists? Do we teach evangelism is for the select few or a responsibility of the whole body?

Pastors must be evangelistic. The gospel message should influence and direct our preaching, prayers, and how we equip the saints for the work of the ministry.

NOURISHMENT FOR THE SOUL

CHILDREN / YOUTH EVANGELISM
Jeffery Jackson

Two of the four Gospels end with the great commission: "Go into all the world and preach the gospel to every creature" (Mark 16:15 NKJV). For this reason, we should take evangelism very seriously, because "what will it profit a man if he gains the whole world, and loses his own soul" (Mark 8:36 NKJV)? Therefore, evangelism is the core of Christianity. Through evangelism, men, women, boys, and girls from all walks of life are given an opportunity to be atoned for their sins through faith in Jesus Christ as their Savior and Lord.

Evangelizing children and youth cannot be taken for granted. Their understanding is dependent upon their background as churched and unchurched. There is certain religious language used when sharing with the churched that has to be simplified for the unchurched. And at times, it takes out-of-the-box thinking and techniques to reach them. But regardless of the technique, the overall goal of children/youth evangelism is for children and youth, churched and unchurched, to come to the awareness of the sinful state of their soul and their need for a Savior who reconciles their connection back to God.

FOCUS GROUP

When it comes to evangelism, we have a tendency to gravitate to the safe places—the good neighborhoods, the prospects who look like us, dress like us, and live like us. But there are many other groups who miss out on hearing about Jesus because of our innate fears, stereotypes, and learned behaviors. To be an effective evangelist, one cannot judge the worthiness of a person to receive salvation by the outward appearance, but one must look deeper at the other's sin-stained soul that God so loved that He gave His only begotten Son to save. Therefore, it is important to not only evangelize where we are comfortable and familiar, but also where we may be uncomfortable and unfamiliar. In the parable of the wedding feast in Matthew 22, the servants went out to the usual crowd and invited them to the wedding feast, but many paid the servants no mind or mistreated them. Then the king told the servants to go to the highways and byways and invite any, and everyone, to the feast. They did so. They went to the highways and byways and invited the good and the bad. We must do the same.

NEED FOR THIS TYPE OF EVANGELISM

Not everyone is going to jump on the bandwagon and go to places that are perceived to be dangerous or high risk for violence and crimes. Others are hesitant to go the places of poverty. Therefore, in such places, darkness and hopelessness seem to prevail. From a distance, we preach that such neighborhoods need the presence of Jesus, but we don't want to get directly involved. We hear the cries of the people, "Lord, have mercy!" But we either ignore the cries or we refuse to make room for them in our hearts.

Or we might even say that the risk is too high. The overhead to support impoverished families will hurt the ministry. Poor people can't help the church money-wise. We will be giving more than we take in. We forget God's promise to bless us abundantly so that in all things at all times, having all we need, we will abound in every good work. So the people in the most undesirable places lose hope. The children see no way out of the dark abyss where light is absent. They also lose purpose. And without hope and purpose, the children have nothing to lose. They join gangs, participate in criminal activities, and harm others and themselves. Many of them die without ever hearing about the One who loves them and wants them to prosper and succeed on this side of life, and who wants them to spend eternity with Him in the hereafter. For this cause, we *must* go to all the world—the "perceived" good places and the so-called bad—and preach the gospel to every creature.

THE GREAT EXCHANGE

Every day during the summer, from around 4:00 p.m. until sunset, a group of young men play basketball in the parking lot of a local church on one of the busiest streets in my neighborhood. One day on my way home from work, as I observed the packed parking lot and the full courts, the Holy Spirit spoke to me and said, "The harvest is plentiful."

At first, I tried to pretend I didn't hear the Spirit. But each day, He kept reminding me of the harvest that was right before my eyes, begging to be picked. I was hesitant about approaching the young men; several years earlier, there had been a shooting at those same courts. A gunman had targeted one of the players, so I didn't know what kind of crowd congregated at the court. Also, I didn't know how to approach them. I had not played basketball in a very long time, so I knew I wasn't about to ask to join in on one of their games. In order for me to go as the Spirit prompted, I had to think outside the box. I prayed, and the Lord blessed me with an idea. He said that during the hot summer afternoons, the young men will be thirsty and hungry. Go buy some variety pack chips and small bottles of Gatorade and water and put them on ice. Take them to the court. Make an announcement that the young men may have the drinks and the chips in exchange for ten minutes of their time.

I did as the Spirit guided. One summer morning, I purchased chips, Gatorade, and water. I put the Gatorade and water on ice. That afternoon on the way home, I drove by and saw the crowd in the parking lot. I went home, changed clothes, packed up my "bargaining chips," gathered my tools for evangelism, and went.

I arrived while a game was in progress. I parked, took the chips and cooler out of the trunk, and placed them in a visible place so that when the game was over, I could grab everyone's attention before they started another game. There were a couple of young men in their car waiting for their turn to play. One yelled from the car, "Is that for us? Is it free?"

I replied, "After the game, if you all give me ten minutes of your time, then you can have it all."

So after the game, I made the proposition to the rest of the players. In exchange for ten minutes of their undivided attention, they would receive ice-cold Gatorade, water, and chips. They gladly put down the basketball and gathered around.

For ten minutes, I shared the gospel using t-shirts—a technique that the Spirit had led me to use a year prior, which led to the conversion of many youths. I shared the redemption story from the beginning with the creation of man to the death, burial, and resurrection of Jesus Christ. I used a brown t-shirt to represent the dirt from which man was created. I used a white t-shirt to represent the soul of man before the fall of Adam and Eve. I used a black t-shirt to represent sin that covered the soul after Adam and Eve disobeyed God. I used an apple to represent the fruit from the tree. I used a red t-shirt to represent the blood of Jesus that washes away sin. I used a yellow t-shirt to represent the light that we are to let shine after our souls have been saved by the blood of Jesus.

It was a hot summer afternoon, so slipping the t-shirts on and off was a little uncomfortable, but it was worth it. The message stuck with the young men. At the end of the story, they knew that they needed the blood of Jesus to cover their sins. I prayed the prayer of salvation, and five young men joined in and openly prayed to receive Christ. One even asked what church I attended and where it was located. The message of Jesus had clearly made an impression upon him.

During basketball season, our local church hosts basketball for children and youth who live in various cities throughout the Memphis metropolitan area. As part of the program, before the teams play, a guest speaker talks to them about life beyond basketball. When I was invited to speak one Saturday morning, I spoke to the teens not only about life beyond basketball but also about life beyond death. Having the teens' undivided attention, I could not pass up this opportunity to share the gospel of salvation. For fifteen minutes, I shared the gospel using the same tool I used for the young men in the church's parking lot. At the end of the presentation, three teens gave their lives to Christ. They left for the day victorious, regardless of whether they won the basketball game or not.

Two years after the presentation, a young man came up to me. I did not recognize him, but he recognized me and shared with me his remembrance of the t-shirt presentation and what each color meant. My heart rejoiced that the presentation had made such an impression upon him that he still remembered the details two years later.

To learn more about spreading the gospel with the t-shirt presentation, visit https://youtu.be/sTjmKawuVqg for the presentation using actual t-shirts and https://youtu.be/snWKeG_w-yI for the presentation using the T-shirt Gospel Kit.

The harvest is plentiful. God has blessed us with His Holy Spirit to give us the courage and creativity to reach not only those in our traditional settings but also those in the highways and byways.

MEETING THEM WHERE THEY ARE

It is our tradition to meet on Sunday at the church building. We fellowship and encourage one another (Hebrews 10:25). We sing songs of praise to the Lord (Ephesians 5:19). We share how thankful we are for all God has done, especially in saving our souls (Psalm 100). And we pity those who do not know Jesus—the many who will meet their doom on the day of judgement. Yet we do nothing about it except hope they come and join us in our buildings on Sunday morning.

The evangelistic team at our church came up with the idea to take one Sunday off from gathering at the building and, instead, go out into the community during the regular church hour. Rather than simply pitying those who might be destined for doom and hoping they would join us at church service, we decided to go from house to house and proclaim the good news of the gospel to them instead.

Taking a small team, we partnered up one Sunday morning and went door knocking. Since the majority of "churched" folks were in church buildings, we knew that our chances of reaching the "unchurched" were high. Our first encounter was a teenager. He had just gotten out of bed, and his parents were not home. We explained who we were and asked if he had a moment to chat. Surprisingly, he invited us into his home.

As we sat with him, we talked about school and other things important to young people. We finally got around to talking about God,

Heaven, and Jesus, and we used a survey to keep the discussion going. One of our last questions was, "Do you believe it's important that a person knows how to go to heaven?"

The young man said that it was important. Then we went on to ask him about his relationship with God. When he said he went to church, we explained to him that there was more to being saved than just going to church. We asked if he would like to be certain that his soul was saved and would spend eternity in Heaven. After we shared the gospel with him using the Evangecube evangelism tool (https:// e3resources.org/), he accepted Christ as Savior and Lord. We wrote down his address and later forwarded him more information about the decision he had made.

Sometimes, we have to go out into the field and pick the harvest instead of waiting for the harvest to come to us. And what a harvest it is! The probability is higher that you will reach an unbeliever at home on Sunday morning than any other time. Go ye into all the world, even on Sunday morning!

THE NEXT LEVEL

Once I paid a visit to a teenager at one of the children's hospitals in Memphis. The young lady, who was turning seventeen, had suffered from juvenile diabetes since age twelve. Wanting desperately to live normal like every other teen, the young lady neglected her diet and did not watch her sugar level. Several times a month, she was admitted into the hospital because she allowed her sugar level to get to a critical state and only the hospital could get her stabilized. At the same time, she was destroying healthy organs in her body.

Normally, we would pray for the patient and be on our way. But there are times when we take our visits to the next level. This was one of the cases. I took down contact information about the patient and was determined to make a home visit after the patient was discharged. Simply following the prompting of the Holy Spirit, I did not realize the journey ahead of me.

When I decided to make a visit, I mapped the address and discovered the apartment complex was in what some might consider an unsafe neighborhood. When I arrived, I was introduced to the rest of the family—the young lady's siblings and her mother. The family's home was neat and orderly, but one thing lacking was the proper food for someone with diabetes. Through a dietitian, a health plan was developed for the teen, and some of the foods she needed was supplied. So through months of visiting and caring for the teen, we ended up meeting the needs of the entire family in various ways. There were many ups and downs, especially with the young lady with diabetes. Unfortunately, she did not change her mind about wanting to live a normal life. She neglected herself again and again and was frequently admitted to the hospital. One day, when she was admitted, the Holy Spirit prompted me to speak to her about her spiritual condition. I explained to her that God loved her so much that He wanted her to become a part of His family. After I shared the gospel with her, she accepted Jesus as her Savior.

Over the next few years, the young lady still struggled with properly managing her diabetes. One evening, I received a call that she was on life support. All her vital organs had failed. I was there with the family as we gathered and prayed, more for the family than for the young lady. We watched as the medical staff resuscitated her three times. But she did not survive. Because we had taken our care for the young lady to the next level and was able to reach her soul, though she was absent from the body she hated so much, she was present with the Lord.

Now, whenever I am called to the hospital to pray for a sick person, I always pray first for their salvation, then for their physical healing. And whenever possible, I try to minister to the entire family and not just the one who is physically ill. Every soul, regardless of the situation, circumstance, or place, is precious to God. If we are prompted to go, then we should go and leave the consequences to God.

NOURISHMENT FOR THE SOUL

CALL-BASED EVANGELISM
Allen R. Grimes

The privilege of being chosen by God to do His work has great rewards. This reward comes with marching orders that require discipline and sacrifice from those He has chosen. The love shown to us involves living out the gospel, sharing the gospel, and winning souls for him. Jesus says to His disciples, "You did not choose Me, but I chose you and appointed you that you should go and bear fruit" (John 15:16).

Call-Based Evangelism is following God's lead in your life while imparting to others the message and teachings of Jesus Christ. This calling is not about a title, but more about the assignment. God chooses those who stand for Him. Jesus says, "For many are called, but few are chosen" (Matthew 20:16).

The calling can be evident as a disciple of Jesus Christ, but a chosen disciple with His purpose in mind stands out when genuinely led by God. Call-Based Evangelism is setting aside yourself unto God whereby others witnessing His work in you become saved. There is a need for the world to see God working in His disciples as they choose to serve Him and others.

I have longed to serve God and His people all my life. I was born in Memphis, Tennessee, and reared in church for as long as I can remember. The example of my parents and people in the church showing God's love toward others stood out the most. This passion flowed into my life as an adult. I recall God working in my life as a young man as I served as the youngest deacon at Holman Street Baptist Church in Houston, Texas. Not knowing what to expect, I trusted my love for God to lead me in this new direction.

Serving at Holman Street reminded me of Romans 12:11, where one must be "not lagging in diligence, fervent in spirit, serving the Lord." God used my wife and me tremendously to serve God and His

17

people. We became new members' orientation teachers, which required us to study God's Word more than we ever had. We participated in the Soul Winning Action Committee (SWAC), an evangelistic effort that allowed us to share the Gospel of Jesus Christ to people of all walks of life in the Third Ward community of Houston, Texas.

Following God became easy, but understanding God's plan was another thing. With a toddler boy sent by God, a new house, a great church family, what could be better? God would lead us on another journey that would strengthen our faith even more. We would leave all we had in Houston, Texas, and move to Silver Spring, Maryland.

Upon our arrival to Maryland, God would grace us with another child. A beautiful baby girl. This movement of God's spirit would eventually lead to my call to preach the Gospel of Jesus Christ. At first, thinking this move was for business, God continued to use my family and me for His Kingdom. I would soon be ordained as a preacher to conduct the ministry of Evangelism at Faith Community Baptist Church in Silver Spring, Maryland. At this point, Call-Based Evangelism is taking its root.

The assignment was becoming more apparent. Serving as an associate minister, I witnessed the Gospel of Jesus Christ to many in the community. The study of God's Word was the delight of my life. Sharing that Word would become my passion. Whenever I could teach and preach His Word, I would. I taught and preached to men, boys, women, and girls; it did not matter.

This part of Call-Based Evangelism reminds me of how God puts us in a position to be used for Him and by Him. Paul says it like this, "And we know that all things work together for good to those who love God, to those who are the called according to His purpose" (Romans 8:28). The passion for serving God and His people did not stop here.

God led me to start a community Bible Study, which eventually turned into Harvest Time Community Church. I would serve as the Senior Pastor of a primarily African American Bible-based ministry. Many people would come to know Jesus as their Lord and Savior.

Again, God would choose me for another assignment. One that would challenge my faith and those who I served. After seven years of great ministry at Harvest Time, God would ask me what the next seven years would be. How could His people see Him more? Our church merged with a multi-cultural church with people from nations worldwide. The pastor of First Alliance Church and myself became a pastoral team that is better together. God would change our outlook on how the Kingdom of God should be. Our community of believers is forever changed! We began to see the Gospel of Jesus Christ not as a territorial gospel but a worldwide gospel.

This merger is just the beginning of what Call-Based Evangelism truly stands for. It's being obedient to the call of God in Matthew 28:19 to "Go therefore and make disciples of all the nations, baptizing them in the name of the Father and of the Son and of the Holy Spirit." The lesson from Call-Based Evangelism is to follow God's lead to reach souls for Christ.

THE FIVE P'S OF EFFECTIVE EVANGELISM: PREPARE, PINPOINT, PERSONALIZE, PICTURIZE, AND PRESCRIBE

(In this book, *Sharing the Gospel, Good News on the Go*, medical terms are used to relate biblical truths and to convey the plan of salvation).

I. ***Prepare:*** The soul winner must be prepared to refer the patient to the Great Physician for healing.

   The soul winner is an intern who tells the patient what the doctor can and will do to him, for him, with him, and through him.

II. ***Pinpoint:*** The soul winner must keep the patient's attention focused on Jesus Christ.

   The soul winner is a Paramedic who is trained to take the patient's vital signs, analyze the patient's condition, and transport the patient to the Great Physician for medical treatment.

III. ***Personalize:*** The soul winner's consultation must be made real to the patient's heart condition.

   The soul winner is the Nurse who prepares the patient and the atmosphere for an appointment with the Great Physician, Jesus. The nurse assesses the patience's signs and symptoms both verbal and non-verbal. Additionally, the nurse provides psychological and emotional support, as the patient awaits an appointment with the Great Physician, Jesus.

IV. ***Picturize:*** The soul winner must paint a description of hope in the mind of the patient.

   The soul winner is a Therapist who advises the patient of his condition, encourages him during rehabilitation, monitors the patient's progress, and assists the patient in following the Great Physician's orders for complete restoration and recovery.

V. **Prescribe:** The soul winner informs the patient that the best prescription for his condition can only be administered by the Great Physician.

The soul winner is the Pharmacist who fills the prescription according to the doctor's orders. When the patient's condition changes and warrants refills, the Pharmacist advises the patient to contact the Great Physician. Sin is a disease that requires prescriptions that can only be written and prescribed by the Great Physician.

Jesus is the divine treatment plan, cure, and remedy for the world's greatest ailment—sin.

NOURISHMENT FOR THE SOUL

THE RESTROOM WITNESS
Matthew A. Davis

Don't think outside the box. Think like there is no box.
—Ziad K. Abdelnour

The month of April was the designated period for Evangelism Emphasis, Street Preaching, and Spring Revival at the Holman Street Missionary Baptist Church in Houston, Texas. The year of 1995 was no exception. One night after a very fruitful revival, the pastor, the evangelist, and the associate ministers went to Kim Son's Restaurant downtown to share in fellowship and a good meal. The drinks, water and tea that is, were being served and the conversation at the table was turned to that of review, critique, and results of our soul-winning experiences. We thanked God for the souls reached. We prayed for the harvest of the day. And we asked God to bless our efforts for the rest of the revival time.

Then it happened. I excused myself from the table and the fellowship to go to the restroom. Upon arriving in the restroom, armed with my Four Spiritual Laws tracts of course, I noticed a young man standing in the restroom, facing the wall. You see, ladies, it is not unusual to find several men in the restroom facing the wall. That is just what we do. Ninety-eight percent of the men in the restrooms across America are standing facing the walls. The men's restrooms do not have the extravagances that one may find in the women's restrooms. There are no chairs, no tables, no couches, no beautiful flower arrangements, nor loveseats in the men's restrooms. I stood right next to him, facing the wall. Sure, all things were normal—two men in the men's restroom, standing facing the wall. Please remember, I am armed with my Four Spiritual Laws tracts and I am ready! I know for a fact, once a man gets started, it is difficult, damaging, and virtually impossible for a man to stop midstream. Wow, God has set me up. He has placed the two of us in the midst of a divine appointment. I patiently waited for the perfect moment for me to begin my homiletical presentation of the Gospel of Jesus the Christ.

The communication went kind of like this:" Have you heard of the Four Spiritual Laws?"

His first thought obviously was, "Why are you talking to me in the restroom?"

Men just do not spend time talking in the restroom. But without an answer from him, I proceeded. He begins to nod, "Yes." This was an indication that I should continue. So I did.

THE FOUR SPIRITUAL LAWS

(Bright, The Four Spiritual Laws, 1994)[1]

Law 1: "God loves you and offers a wonderful plan for your life" (John 3:16).
Law 2: "Man is sinful and separated from God" (Romans 3:23).
Law 3: "God demonstrates His love by Jesus' death and resurrection for our sins" (Romans 5:8; 1 Corinthians 15:3–6).
Jesus is the only one who can connect us to God.
Law 4: "You must receive Him (Jesus) for yourself by placing our faith in Jesus" (John 1:12; Ephesians 2:8–9).

By now I knew that the iron was hot, so I asked the question. Would you like to invite Christ in your life right now? He answered, yes. I led him in the prayer, and he received Christ, standing facing the wall. Hallelujah to God for saving another soul! Some people, even seminary students, have stated that there is a time and a place for everything. So, they ask, "Was that the right time and the right place?" My reply is always the same: If people cry, talk, lie, and gossip in the restroom, why can't or wouldn't we win souls in the restroom?

The situation is critical!
The message is urgent!
We must witness!

---

[1] http://www.4laws.com/laws/englishkgp/default.htm

NOURISHMENT FOR THE SOUL

THE WITNESS
The Courtroom Scene
Matthew A. Davis and Sharon Booker

PROSECUTOR: Would you state your name for the record, please?

WITNESS: Sharon Booker

PROSECUTOR: Do you swear to tell the truth, the whole truth, and nothing but the truth, so help you God?

WITNESS: I do.

PROSECUTOR: Sister Booker, it is rumored that you believe in this man called Jesus Christ; is that correct?

WITNESS: That is true.

PROSECUTOR: Sister Booker, it is also rumored that you believe that Jesus died and yet he rose; is that correct?

WITNESS: That is correct.

PROSECUTOR: Sister Booker, where did you get such information?

WITNESS: I got my information from the Word of God, which is the Bible.

PROSECUTOR: The Bible?

WITNESS: Yes.

PROSECUTOR: Which Bible is that?

WITNESS: There is only one true Bible. The Bible that was inspired of God and written of men. It is the word of truth. The Bible has 100 percent accuracy.

PROSECUTOR: Sister Booker, you told me that you swear to tell the truth, the whole truth, and nothing but the truth.

WITNESS: That is correct.

PROSECUTOR: And now you're saying that the Bible was inspired by God, written by men?

WITNESS: That is correct.

PROSECUTOR: And you believe that stuff; huh?

WITNESS: Yes, sir, I do.

PROSECUTOR: Why do you believe that, Sister Booker?

WITNESS: Because God told me so.

PROSECUTOR: God told you so?

WITNESS: Yes.

PROSECUTOR: Where?

WITNESS: In his Word.

PROSECUTOR: In his Word where?

WITNESS: His Word is the Bible. His Word is the Bible.

PROSECUTOR: The Bible?

WITNESS: Yes.

PROSECUTOR: Which Bible is that?

WITNESS: The Bible that I just described to you, one that you had me to place my hand on and say do I tell the whole truth and nothing but the truth, so help me God.

PROSECUTOR: Is that right, Sister Booker?

WITNESS: Yes

PROSECUTOR: Sister Booker, it is also rumored that you are saved by grace.

WITNESS: Yes, that is true.

PROSECUTOR: Can you explain that to the court, please?

WITNESS: Yes, I can explain that, sir. I am saved by faith through Jesus Christ and not of myself. It is a gift of God. It is God's gift to man, "For God so loved the world that he gave his only begotten Son that whosoever would believe in him should not perish but should have everlasting life" (John 3:16). God commended his love toward me while I was yet a sinner (Romans 5:8). He died for me on the cross. He came into this world that I might be saved. And therefore, it is a gift of grace because it is something that I could not have done for myself; yet it was a gift that God gave, and Jesus Christ paid it all. He paid the price on the cross.

PROSECUTOR: Now, I guess since you are the witness and I am the prosecutor, I guess you're about to tell me this is what I ought to believe also.

WITNESS: Yes, sir, I'm going to say that this is not only what you ought to believe, but I'm also going to say that, sir, I perceive that you are a man of great intelligence, and I believe that you are a man that's looking…

PROSECUTOR: You're right about that.

WITNESS: You are a man who is looking for the truth. I gather that you are a man who looks for fact and not fiction.

PROSECUTOR: That's true! (arrogantly)

WITNESS: I perceive, sir, that you will reach out and search for yourself. So I compel you right now, sir, to search the scriptures, to see for yourself and not to take my word but the word of others that have seen Jesus and know who he is. Even after he died, he showed himself to many; and that is described to us in this book that you kept asking me about, the book that you yourself asked me to place my hand on, the book that tells us who Jesus is, why he came, how he came, and what he will do for us (1 Corinthians 15:1–5). Sir, I believe this, and I believe that you should believe. I believe that if you accept the Lord Jesus Christ as your personal savior, that he will save you. I believe that salvation is twofold. I believe that God works, and man believes. I believe that God did the work at Calvary, but yet he left something for us to do, and that is that we would believe on the Lord Jesus Christ. I believe in the "Isness" of God. I believe that God is the way, the truth, and the light. I believe that God is the Alpha and the Omega. I trust that the only way to God is through his son Jesus Christ. I believe that Jesus came that we might have life and that we might have it more abundantly. Sir, I perceive that you are a man of great intelligence, and I distinguish that you are a man that is seeking after the truth. I also believe that you are a man who is missing something in your life, and you are searching for it in the wrong places. I discern that you are trying to fill a void that only God can fill in your life. God made man so that he could live happily with him in Heaven.

God made man so that he could have eternal life and live with him. And, sir, I perceive that you are one whom God would love to have on his side, walking with him. Sir, I know you want to know how you can get to know this man. Well, let me explain that to you if I may, Mr. Prosecutor. There is only one way to get to know him, and that is first to be in a right relationship with Jesus Christ. And how do you do that, sir? How do you come into this relationship? Well, first, you must know your position. The position of every man that is without Christ is that he is a sinner. He does not know God. There's a gap, and because of that gap, we cannot come to God. We have to have a way to get to God. That gap is filled with sin. See, the first man, Adam, sinned. But thanks be to God, the second man, Jesus Christ, came to take that sin nature away from man. So, sir, you need to believe in your heart, first, you are a sinner. It is nothing you can do of yourself. Then the second thing you need to know is that you can be saved. Yes, you can be saved. Just as sure as it's a fact that you are a sinner, it is a fact that God loves you. God loves you beyond anything that you could ever think or imagine. Well, now, how do I know that? I know that because John—

PROSECUTOR: Yeah, how do you know that?

WITNESS: John 3:16 says: "For God so loved the world that he gave his only begotten son that whosoever would believe in him would not perish but could have everlasting life." I tell you that God loves you with a love that you could never imagine. God loves you with a love so much that he would give something so precious to him as his son, and that his son would take on the form of man, not because that is what he needed to do, but that's what he wanted to do so that you and I could understand him, so that we could be touched by what he has to say. He could have come in any form, but he chose the form of a lowly man just as you and me so that he could be on the level where we are, and he could reach us, and he could raise us up to the level where he wanted us to be. He could not come in any other way. And not only does God love

31

you, not only is it a fact that you can be saved, but it is also a fact that all you must do right now is to accept Christ, and that's all you have to do. The Bible says, "If thou confess with thy mouth and believe with thine heart the Lord Jesus Christ, thou shalt be saved," thou will be saved (Romans 10:9–10). I said earlier to you that salvation is twofold. Salvation is God working on the behalf of man, but he leaves something for you and me to do, for he knows that we are people of great intellect. See, God is not a man that he will tell a lie. You and I are men, we tell lies. But God is not a man; He will not tell us a lie. God put himself in us. Therefore, he gave us will, intellect, and sensibility. Mr. Prosecutor, I ask are you ready to accept the Lord Jesus Christ and be saved?

PROSECUTOR: How do I accept Jesus Christ?

WITNESS: All you have to do is to accept Jesus Christ in your heart is believe in your heart and confess with your mouth through a simple prayer. Say, "Lord, I know I'm a sinner and I believe that you sent your Son to die on the cross for me. I believe that He is the Son of God, and I accept him in my life as my personal savior. And I want Him to be ruler in my life."

PROSECUTOR: I believe it, Lord.

WITNESS: And I accept You in my life right now as my personal savior.

PROSECUTOR: I thank you, Lord! I thank for saving me! Now, Lord, send me to a church, where I can know more about Jesus! I want to be taught more about Jesus! Then, I can become a witness for Him. It is in the precious name of Jesus that I pray. Amen.

WITNESS: Welcome to the Family of God, Brother!

NOURISHMENT FOR THE SOUL

CHAPTER 1
Prepare

The soul winner must be prepared to refer the patient to the Great Physician for healing.

The soul winner is an *Intern* who tells the patient what the Doctor can and will do to him, for him, with him, and through him.

Since every soul is vitally important to God, the winning of a soul is considered an emergency for the *Intern* (the Soul Winner). The greatest miracle that one will ever experience is the saving of a lost soul.

The soul winner must have already experienced salvation to effectively witness for Jesus Christ. Jesus said to Nicodemus in John 3:3 that "…except a man be born again he cannot see the kingdom of God." This process of "Seeing the Kingdom" can only be perceived through the spiritual eyes (1 Corinthians 2:14). Therefore, the soul winner must be born of the spirit of God to carry out the great commission (Matthew 28:18–20), and to identify with teachings presented in this book.

THE SALVATION STORY

Dorothy just told her new classmate Alex, a non-Christian, that he does not have to run, jump, scream, or shout to be saved. She explains that salvation comes from what Jesus has already done and not of anything we have done. It's just that simple. If you confess with your mouth and believe with your heart, you can be saved (Romans 10:9–10). Dorothy invites Alex to accept Jesus now.

Classroom Activity:

Ask for two volunteers to play Dorothy and Alex in the following exercise.

Dorothy: Alex, you can be saved right here, right now, today.

Alex: How? You mean I don't have to go to church first and listen to
the preacher?

Dorothy: You can accept Jesus into your life right now by simply believing
that Jesus is the Son of God. Do you believe this, Alex?

Alex: Yes.

Dorothy: Do you believe that Jesus died and rose for your sins?

Alex: Yes. Now what?

Dorothy: Invite Jesus into your heart to be your Savior. Repeat after me, Alex.

Dorothy prays the sinner's prayer as Alex repeats after her. The Prayer of Salvation "Dear God, I thank you for this privilege to pray. God, *I am a sinner.* I ask that you *forgive me* of my sins. I believe that

Jesus is your son. I believe that *He died* for my sins. I believe *He was buried* in a borrowed tomb. I believe on the third day, *He rose* from the dead. Now, God, I invite Jesus into my life. God, fill me with your Holy Spirit. In Jesus's name I pray, Amen" (1 Corinthians 15:1–5).

Those who pray this prayer while believing in his heart shall be saved now (Romans 10:9–10).

A SOUL WINNER'S TOOL KIT

Jesus Christ is always the main attraction in the witnessing encounter. A witness should never focus on anyone or anything other than Jesus Christ and His saving power. You must witness in the Spirit—be guided and led by the anointing power of the Holy Spirit. Therefore, it is imperative that you spend time seeking God through His word and praying daily in order to be an effective witness. As a soul winner, you should spend 90 percent of your time in Bible study, prayer, and meditation and 10 percent of your time actually "sharing the gospel."

John 6:44a proclaims, "No man can come to me, except the Father which hath sent me draw him." This passage of scripture places responsibility on the soul winner to simply present the gospel truth. The focus is not on your personal conversion experience, current events, catchy phrases, or the latest gossip. Only the Gospel of Jesus's death, burial, and resurrection will *"turn hearts toward God."*

A soul winner is always prepared to be a witness. Here are some tips you may adopt in *preparation* for the delivery:

- *Journal.* Keep a journal and record your devotional periods. Write your thoughts and ideas down as the Holy Spirit brings things to your remembrance.
- *Bible Study.* Study and meditate on the Word of God daily.
- *Prayer.* Pray daily and beseech the anointing presence and power of the Holy Spirit. The circumstances and challenges of life cause us to participate in a consistent prayer life.
- *Consecration.* Decide on a regular time to pray. Designate a specific place to dedicate your heart faithfully and consistently to God and meditate on His word daily.
- *Devotion.* Write things down for your memory bank. Study the Word of God. Pray over the Word of God daily. Pray the Word of God. Be prepared to take advantage of any witnessing opportunities God reveals to you through your environment, relationships, and circumstances.

A cardiovascular specialist studies for several years in order to specialize in his field. As he performs one major procedure after another, his success rate increases. He becomes a world-renowned specialist in his field. He knows that the life or death of a patient is dependent on how well he *prepares* himself before surgery. Likewise, it should be with a soul winner. Similarly, you must be spiritually *prepared* to witness to sin sick patients. What you say and how you say it can impact whether the patient inherits eternal life or eternal death (damnation). Therefore, the *preparation* stage is the single most important aspect of the soul winning process.

Scripture gives us several methods of evangelism. Winning souls is a serious matter and should be approached with the leading of the Holy Spirit. The following scriptures give leverage for these methods. Consider the following when attempting to share the gospel with others.

1. Serving according to Acts 9: Dorcas
2. Invitational according to John 4: Woman at the Well
3. Interpersonal or Relational according to Luke 5: Matthew's Party
4. Testimonial according to John 9: Blind Man
5. Intellectual according to Acts 17: Paul at Athens
6. Confrontational according to Acts 2: Peter's Sermon[2]

---

[2] file:///C:/Users/mattd/Downloads/SixEffectiveEvangelisticStyles-adaptedfromBecomingaContagiousChristian042114%20(1).pdf

PRAYER EVANGELISM
Pam Lilly

Prayer evangelism is exercising the power of prayer in the spread of the Gospel through petitions to God for people to accept the Good News and receive the gift of God's grace in the person of Jesus Christ. It also involves praying for the opportunity to be used by God in the salvation process. Therefore, prayer plays a significant part in evangelism and is essential to the work of an evangelist.

Prayer evangelism is equally an individual and globally inclusive approach focused on the world, nations, and people groups. God's love for the world (John 3:16) and Christ's commission to go to all nations (Matthew 28:19) and people groups call for an all-encompassing prayer evangelism strategy. And because prayer transcends boundaries and the role of the Holy Spirit operating at the personal level, we can efficiently pray for everyone's salvation.

It is not God's desire for any to perish (2 Peter 3:9b), so praying the will of the Father puts us in agreement with His desire. Therefore, we have but to participate in God's will for a person's salvation by praying. God declares in Revelations 3:20, "Here I am! I stand at the door and knock. If anyone hears my voice and opens the door, I will come in and eat with that person, and they with me" (NIV). Our role as disciples of Christ is to pray as God knocks at the door of a person's heart, that they hear His voice and open the door of their heart and receive Him.

God has committed us to the message and ministry of reconciliation. We see this explained in 2 Corinthians 5:18–19 when Paul says to the Corinthians believers, "All this is from God, who reconciled us to Himself through Christ and gave us the ministry of reconciliation: that God was reconciling the world to Himself in Christ, not counting men's trespasses against them. And He has committed to us the message of reconciliation" (NIV). Our commitment to the work and message of reconciliation begins with prayer.

In John 17:20, Jesus models praying for those who are yet to believe in Him when he prays, "I am praying not only for these disciples but also for all who will ever believe in me through their message" (NLT). As followers of Jesus, we also pray for those who have not yet placed their faith in Christ. We cannot convince a person to put their trust in Jesus Christ. This is the work of the Holy Spirit. We can share the message of the Gospel, but it is the Holy Spirit that does the work in their hearts.

Another effective way to engage in prayer evangelism is to join the work of missionaries serving in foreign countries through prayer. We can pray for the missionaries' well-being and safety in faraway places. And we can also pray for the people group those missionaries are evangelizing. To offer up prayers of intercession as missionaries do the work of sharing the Gospel energizes their work. "This is the confidence we have in approaching God: that if we ask anything according to his will, he hears us" (1 John 5:14 (NIV).

Our prayer is that the Holy Spirit will prepare their heart to receive the message gladly when it is shared. Prayer for the unsaved can be for a specific individual or a nation of people. It is a privilege to join God in the salvation effort by praying for the souls of those we know personally, whether a family member, friend, or someone you have never met. Prayer evangelism is useful when you become aware that a person has not accepted Jesus as their Savior.

We can pray and ask God to allow us to be a part of sharing the Gospel with a person and to give us opportunities to have spiritual conversations with people seeking to know about Jesus. At the very least, ask to be a part of sharing the Good News with those who are still far from Him. And if not you, pray that God would bring someone into their life who is willing to tell them about Jesus.

Like links in a chain, you can be a part of connecting a person to the Truth about God's love for them. But regardless of the role you physically play, prayer plays a significant part in a person's salvation. I pray

- that the Holy Spirit would move them into a relationship with Jesus Christ;
- for the courage to speak up when God presents the opportunity to share His great act of love;
- for the boldness of other Christians to share Jesus with those they encounter throughout their day;
- for the right words to say to individuals who need to put their faith in Jesus Christ;
- for sensitivity to the leading of the Holy Spirit in these matters because a person's eternal life hangs in the balance;
- that the unsaved will believe and put their trust in what Jesus has already done for them.

We rub shoulders with people all the time who are walking in darkness and living without hope. We can ask God to point them out to us and be ready to share our story and His story when he does. Then lead them to pray the Salvation prayer, repenting for their sins, accepting the debt that Jesus has already paid on the cross, and confessing Jesus Christ is Lord. Finally, have them invite Jesus to come into their heart and live with them all the days of their lives.

Then begin praying for this new brother or sister in Christ. "Therefore, if anyone *is* in Christ, he is a new creation; old things have passed away; behold, all things have become new" (2 Corinthians 5:17 NKJV). Pray that,

- they will be strong and grow in their faith in Christ Jesus and walk with Him daily.
- God will surround them with strong Christians to disciple them in their faith.
- they will connect them with a Bible-believing church to hear the Word of God taught and preached.
- they will read the Bible and grow in the knowledge of God's Word.
- their faith will remain strong and courageous when adversity comes.

Prayer evangelism starts, concludes, and then continues with prayer. You continue to pray for this new believer every time the Holy Spirit brings them to your mind. It's not every day that this honor is bestowed upon a follower of Christ, but it makes a lasting impact that you can treasure when it does.

Additional Story:
Journal Entry 7/21/17 (Name Changed)

When God has a planned encounter to rescue a soul, delays and diversions are just a part of His divine plan. As I sat in the center seat of the airplane next to the beautiful little Chloe, I had no idea God would have me lead her to Christ.

It all began when I opened my iPad to work on a jigsaw puzzle. I asked seven-year-old Chloe, who was traveling alone if she liked puzzles. She immediately engaged with me and started helping me with the puzzle. Piece after piece was placed in its proper place until the whole puzzle was complete, and we were both grinning in delight. She was indeed a lover of puzzles, just like she said. She worked one cute animal puzzle after another. I would challenge her to do more difficult puzzles with more pieces each time. She assured me that she couldn't do a hundred-piece puzzle by herself, but she did. She was so pleased with herself.

Chloe's grandmother, whom she lives with, put her on the plane to spend a couple of weeks with her aunt in Denver. About two-thirds of the way there, I asked Chloe if she attended church. She said they don't go to church, but she sometimes went with a neighborhood friend before they moved away and that she liked it.

I asked her if she knew Jesus, and she shook her head no. I began to tell her how someone introduced me to Jesus when I was seven years old, and Chloe was all ears. She intently listened as I told her how much Jesus loves children and He welcomes them to come to Him. I told her about the price Jesus paid for our sin so we could have a relationship with God. I explained how she could know God and how Jesus could live in her heart. Chloe listened to my every word, and she looked me in the eyes and then agreed she wanted to ask Jesus to live in her heart.

I led Chloe in the prayer of salvation to confess her sins and ask Jesus to come into her heart right there in row two. As the pilot announced one delayed landing after another, I told Chloe stories of Jesus and His love for people and His miracles. When our plane got diverted to Amarillo to refuel, I knew it was all a part of God's plan for Chloe to know Him as Lord and Savior.

We talked like two friends, Chloe telling me about her life and me telling her about the love of Jesus. I asked her if she had a Bible, and she said no, but told me her grandmother had a Bible. I told her about children's Bibles. She asked, "Where can I get a children's Bible?" I encouraged her to tell her aunt that she asked Jesus to come and live in her heart and ask her (aunt) if she would get her children's Bible. Then we continued working on puzzles and talking about Jesus and Chloe's new life with Jesus throughout the long delay.

I often pray for Chloe and her new faith in Christ. I pray that she has a Bible she can read and continue to learn more about Jesus. I pray someone will take her to church so she can grow and mature in Christ. I am convinced that God orchestrated me sitting in seat 2E that day, complete with delays and diversions for the sake of Chloe's soul. It never ceases to amaze me the length God will go to for one person's soul.

God had already begun working in Chloe's heart and had even put people in her path to invite her to church. So, I was delighted that God used me to usher Chloe into the Kingdom and welcome her into the family of God.

A PERSON WHO IS ANGRY WITH GOD
Marchelle D. Lee

When considering the scenario in our lesson, we will share some real-life examples of individuals coming to Jesus Christ. Working as a nurse, the souls of my patients and coworkers were as important to me as their physical well-being.

One year after giving my life to Christ, I began working at a local hospital in Cleveland, Ohio, where I made friends with many of the staff there. I had a lot of opportunities to evangelize in this environment. I will share some of my experiences. Twenty-eight years later, we are still friends and living for God.

S. W. was an incredibly angry person. Her nursing techniques and knowledge were remarkable and were greatly commended. However, she was an angry backslider and mad with God, life, her babies' daddy, at the time she had one and was pregnant with another. Her pain came across in her conversation; she was abrasive, harsh, dictatorial, and downright rude at times. Being our Charge Nurse on the night shift, we had to be careful how we approached her at any time.

However, I begin to be extremely nice and helpful with the workload on our shift. She watched as I stopped participating in things that were contrary to God's word. One time she stated, "I am watching you, there are so many hypocrites in the church, I am trying to see if you are for real." I read my Bible during lunch and stayed away from the hospital propagandas, gossip, and politics. The Lord led her to approach me and confide in me about her life, disappointments, and pain. I took her to three scriptures: First, "For we have not a high priest which cannot be touched with the feeling of our infirmities; but was in all points tempted like as we are, yet without sin" (Hebrews 4:15). Secondly, we discussed, "The righteous cry, and the LORD heareth, and delivereth them out of all their troubles. The LORD is nigh unto them that are of a broken heart; and saveth such as be of a contrite spirit" (Psalm 31:17–18). Lastly, we read and found God's promise for her troubled mind. Intense anger often stems from one or two things: unforgiveness of the past or fear of the future. The third scripture spoke volumes to S. W. "For if you forgive other people when they sin against you, your heavenly Father will also forgive you" (Matthew 6:14). S. W. rededicated her life to Christ that night according to Romans 10:9–10. She vowed to come to "that church you go to", as soon as I "Drop this Load" (the baby). She did just that and became one of the finest Sunday School Superintendents that the church had ever had to that point. It was our interpersonal relationship and the Spirit of God that led her to Jesus Christ. However, it was only Jesus that could deal with her "Spiritual Coronary Heart Disease." Only he could clear the blockages in her heart.

Nourishment for the Soul

Write a 15 to 30 line essay about your personal salvation experience. Study the key scriptures listed previously. Choose two scriptures and commit them to memory.

NOURISHMENT FOR THE SOUL

CHAPTER 2
Pinpoint

The soul winner must keep the patient's attention focused on Jesus Christ.

The soul winner is a *Paramedic* who is trained to take the patient's vital signs, analyze the patient's condition, and transport the patient to the Great Physician for medical treatment.

PINPOINT THE PATIENT'S CONDITION WITH PRAYER

Dear God, I am grateful that you have saved my soul. Now, God, bless me to be a good steward by allowing me to share the gospel of Jesus Christ with others. God, keep me focused. Help me remember to keep Jesus the main attraction and the center of attention. Lead me into obedience to the Holy Spirit. In Jesus's Name, Amen.

PINPOINTING THE PATIENT'S VITAL SIGNS

The Opportunity. God is interested in your availability and not your capability. Always be on the lookout for and take advantage of the privileges God grants you to be a witness. Be an opportunist, and allow God to use you to win souls. Do not be dismayed at rejection. God is being rejected, not you. One of Satan's tactics is to create frustration and an atmosphere of chaos. He is the author of confusion. The soul winner cannot overcome the darts of Satan in the flesh. It is a spiritual warfare. The soul winner must walk in the Spirit. Yes, Satan is very good at what he does. But remember this powerful truth: "Greater is He that is in you than he that is in the world" (1 John 4:4).

The Diagnostic Examination. Look, search, scan, diagnose, and examine every opportunity God places before you. Do not attempt to force your way into the patient's heart. Allow God to open the door and walk through it with confidence. Forceful entry into a wounded heart could induce a fatal heart attack (total rejection). Waiting for God to pinpoint the opening into the heart will better ensure a successful outcome.

The Diagnostic Procedure. The effective soul winner must identify the primary procedure and source of recovery. Although the soul winner is not perfect, he or she must remember that his patient is wounded. He or she is searching for an answer to his or her ailment. The soul winner is the Great Physician's assistant. The patient trusts you for a referral to the Great Physician who is Jesus *the* Christ. Only the Great Physician can perform the open-heart surgery.

The Major Surgical Procedure. While performing the major surgical procedure, the Great Physician is in constant communication with his team of technicians. Accordingly, it should be with the soul winner and the unbeliever. Good communication is a major factor in soul winning. Zero in on what God is doing through you to assist in cutting out sin's dominion over a life. Stay alert and carefully observe the unbeliever's condition.

Pinpoint the issues of life that are relevant to the patient's deteriorating condition. Do not be overzealous and overwhelm him with biblical principles and preachy remarks. Remember, you are not acting independently of the Great Physician. You need to remain in close supervision of the Great Physician who has never lost a case!

The On-Going Treatment Plan. A soul winner can share personal testimony as a witnessing tool. It can serve to encourage the newborn child in Christ. However, the best testimony is the salvation story, the story of Jesus Christ. He saves souls and causes men to change. If your patient goes off on another tangent and diverts his attention elsewhere, let him or her talk. Keep in mind that it takes a great deal of courage to confess one's faults to another. Listen attentively and do not interrupt or dismiss what he is saying. Wait until the patient finishes and gently interject and call the patient's attention back to the matter at hand—Jesus Christ. The soul winning Christian should maintain control of the soul winning experience. Do not allow the devil to sabotage your witnessing encounter.

MUSICAL EVANGELISM
Carolyn J. Davis

The definition of Music Evangelism can best be described in our motto: "Reaching Youth for Christ Through Music!" Matthew 28:19 commands us to "...go and make disciples."... God didn't tell us to make a particular age group His disciples. He said to go and make disciples of *all* nations—that means men, women, boys, and girls! The younger the person, the greater the advancements of the kingdom of God! Everyone can relate to music in some way or fashion because music is a universal language. What a wonderful way to reach youth, for Christ through one of the subjects they love the most...*music*!

Music Evangelism is much needed in our communities. The Bible tells us to "Train up a child in the way he should go; and when he is old, he will not depart from it" (Proverbs 22:6). If parents are not saved, then who will train the children? Unsaved parents will train children to be unsaved. If we teach the children to have a love for music, develop a relationship with them, then we can teach them about Jesus, the One who can save their souls. If the children become saved, then they can witness to their parents and possibly lead their parents to Christ.

I am reminded of a troubled first grader who attended a school in a socially disadvantaged low-income community. The little girl's teacher didn't know what to do with her because she always threw temper tantrums when she didn't want to do what she was told to do.

Since I was the music teacher, the first-grade teacher expressed to me her troubles with the little girl. She wanted to keep the little girl from coming to music, a class that the little girl enjoyed. In talking with the teacher, I asked her to give me a chance to talk to the little girl.

At that time, parents were asked to send $2 to school to pay for an instrument called a precorder. Learning to play this instrument would teach the students to read music and jump-start their career in playing musical instruments. The mother of this student had not sent the money to pay for the instrument. So in my meeting with the little girl, I told her I would *give* her a precorder to play. I expressed to her that she would be great and would perform in programs at school and would also go on field trips off campus to perform. I also told her that I would *only* give her the instrument if she listened to her teacher, did her classwork and homework, and stopped the temper tantrums!

Well, let me tell you! That little first grader straightened herself up and became a model first grader and precorder player. She played in programs on and off campus and at other schools, hospitals, nursing homes, festivals, and local churches. After first grade, she advanced to the recorder and later to the xylophones and African drums. She performed with the ensemble until she graduated from sixth grade in that elementary school. During that time while she was still at the school, I started inviting the ensemble to practice at my church on Friday nights!

I thought, *If music can change the heart of a first grader and turn her life around, what would it be like if I brought students together in a summer music camp, taught them to play musical instruments, and introduced them to Jesus?* Well, that is just what I did! I believed that if I got the students hooked on playing music, introduce them to Jesus, their lives would be better, and they would be an asset to the Kingdom of God when they grew up. Music was just the drawing card. My goal was reaching youth for Christ!

When that little first grader graduated from sixth grade, she wanted to continue playing with the group. Because of that little girl's desire, my husband and I co-founded the organization "Turning Hearts Music Ensemble" in which students have an opportunity to come together at our church to learn music and learn about God.

In the summer of 2004, the first summer camp was held in our home. After 2004, the camp was moved to the New Beginning Church, Houston, Texas. In addition to the camp being hosted in Houston, Texas, since 2004, the camp has been hosted in two additional towns in Mississippi, Southaven, and Inverness. Many souls have been saved and baptized because of the Summer Enrichment Music Camps. I thank God for using me to make a difference in the lives of young people through music! Thus, our motto: "Reaching Youth For Christ Through Music!" That is Music Evangelism!

—Carolyn J. Davis
Retired Music Teacher, Houston Independent School District
Co-Founder and Director, Turning Hearts Music Ensemble

ON THE GO EVANGELISM
Richard J. Rose

When I began to frequent the bowling alley many years ago, I met many new acquaintances. Many of those new acquaintances were not Christian in their belief and practice. As I became more involved in the sport of bowling, friendships were developed and strengthened. Many times, there were problems. There were problems between bowlers. Sometimes, bowlers were stressed with problems in the home. There were times when some bowlers were stressed because their game was not what they thought it ought to have been.

The Lord, I believe, had me there for such a time. Many of the bowlers gravitated to me. It seemed that I had become the chaplain of the house. And of course, I would always listen to expressed problems and concerns before offering to coach in the named situations.

Jesus, John reports in John 1:14, was incarnational. John wrote, "He dwelt among us." He was where the people were. He was where the hurting humanity was. He was where the need was. Jesus was where he could help. So must the church be today. Such is my practice. I always want to be where the people are. I always want to be where the need is. I always want to be where hurting humanity is.

Some of the most faithful members of our church family are people that I met and had the privilege to share Christ with at the bowling alley.

There was one that I met that became a close friend. I was introduced to her family and was able to share many hours with them. This lady later became a disciple of Christ and an invaluable member in the church. Her son later followed her to the church and surrendered his life to Christ. But after a few years, he transitioned. When the son died, the father attended the home-going service, gave his life to Christ, and became a very devoted sanctuary servant.

After a few years, the father also transitioned. The mother remained faithful until her health failed and later death. Recently, a daughter has confessed Christ and is presently awaiting baptism. It all began by meeting and befriending people at a bowling alley.

There is an amazing story told in the book of Exodus 19:4–6a. There the man of God, Moses, is instructed to tell the people of God how their God had chosen them as His own and how that God wanted the indigenous people in the land to come to know God as they were able to see God at work blessing and protecting Israel. They were to be God's witnesses. God said, "If they would indeed obey my voice and keep my covenant, you shall be my treasured possession among all peoples, for all the earth is mime; and you shall be to me a kingdom of priests and a holy nation. These are the words that you shall speak to the people of Israel."

It was God's plan to use the people of Israel to demonstrate to the people in the land the good and greatness of God. "God makes Himself known through his people." The Israelites failed. They failed God and the surrounding people. God would have them to be living examples of His love and goodness. They failed.

Many Christians today fail God and those around them by not living as unto the Lord so that those around them might be able to see their good works and glorify God. Many Christians today don't realize the powerful influence God has given to them.

Peter writes in 1 Peter 2:9, "But you are a chosen race, a royal priesthood, a holy nation, a people for His own possession, that you may proclaim the excellences of Him who called you out of darkness into His marvelous light." Think about it! God has made us His personal possession and called for us to be His witnesses.

The bowling alley story is only one of many. In each, it can be told how faithful God is when we do His will of telling others about Him.

One final thought. Sharing the good news of Jesus Christ does not always mean cold turkey. It does not always mean approaching some person at a bus stop or knocking on doors. Nor does it mean always making coworkers uncomfortable in the workplace, though there is workplace witnessing.

In my own experience, the best witnessing in done "On the Go." In so doing, we are carrying out the great commission, "As you go, make disciples of all nations" (Matthew 28:19). Be where the need is. Be approachable. Be where there is hurting humanity. Be where people are troubled. Be where people are struggling. John says, "And the Word became flesh and dwelt among us, and we have seen His glory, glory as of the only Son from the father, full of grace and truth."

LIFESTYLE EVANGELISM
Ayanna Alexis Lynn

Lifestyle Evangelism is an "approach to evangelism characterized by someone demonstrating their faith by their actions in the hope that people around them will be impressed with how God affects that person's life and become a Christian." Matthew 5:16 says, "In the same way, let your light shine before others, that they may see your good deeds and glorify your Father in Heaven." What I love about this scripture in the Bible is the fact that God will get the glory through all the good. The light that's shining in you, you didn't put that light there. God did it, and it's our job as Christian to let our light shine and give God the glory for it. Another fact is the scripture before that. The Bible clearly says, your light is not only for you, but it's for others as well. So I chose lifestyle evangelism for several reasons because God did put a light in me that I am using my lifestyle to put light into others. This is how I knew motivational speaking, encouraging others, and being a leader was my strength due to the light was put inside of me.

Where people can get this wrong is because they get so caught up in their own lifestyle and think they blessed themselves when it was God that placed the light in them. It's easy to get caught up in yourself and start to think that it's you making it all happen and shining the light. How this can be fixed is put the light back on the stand and let it shine. It's not our job to hold on to the light or even wonder why God gave us the light. It's easy to get distracted and forget who put the light in you. You have to be content with what you have and your lifestyle.

I remind myself on a daily basis that things can always be worse than what they are. This puts me in a position where I do not complain; this also puts me in a position where I am not satisfied with where I am in life today. I also understand that God has blessed me and God has the power to let my light shine or turn it off. This is why I will forever keep it on the stand and not hold on to it. It's not my light, it's the light God shines through me so people can see that God is the one controlling my life.

Lifestyle evangelism has already been created. The people have taken this type of evangelism and destroyed it do to of the lifestyle that they live. They destroyed it because of the lack of knowledge. Nowadays, the lifestyle you live is all about to impress people. Because of the light God put in you, you do not have to impress people. People will be impressed by what God is doing in your life. So let the light shine that God has put in you, not your light. Your light can never outshine God's light. God has all the power. You will put yourself in a position where you become depressed, feel overwhelmed, and lonely because you are competing with another light that will always outshine your own light.

A GOOD PERSON WHO THINKS SHE'S SAVED
Marchelle D. Lee

L. V. was another young woman who worked with us. She was married and had three sons. She was kind, gracious, and accommodating whenever possible. L. V. was always seeking a way to "mother us." She was on the lookout for places where she felt we needed to exercise caution. This was because we worked on a surgical trauma unit and many of our patients were admitted with a drug overdose, alcohol inebriation, domestic abuse, gunshot wounds, etc. She had keen insight for the patients that came to the unit.

After about three months of being employed at the hospital, God gave me an opportunity to witness to her. Though an effective team member, L. V. had short patience to a fault and often displayed frustration, doubt, and mistrust. Her marital relationship was not going well, either. I came to understand that she had Spiritual Congestive Heart Failure, only a portion of her heart was working. She had been rejecting God's love and others around her. Joining me for lunch one day, she asked, "What are you reading, Marchelle?" My reply was the "Word of God," and that was an open door. We discussed the fact that she was raised in church, etc. Although she admitted to not having a personal relationship with Christ, she stated, "I think I am a good person, and I try to do the right thing."

Again, this was a great opportunity to share the Word of God. These are the scriptures that we conversed about: "And Jesus said unto him, why callest thou me good? *there is* none good but one, *that is*, God" (Mark 10:18). "Behold, I was shapen in iniquity; and in sin did my mother conceive me. Behold, thou desirest truth in the inward parts: and in the hidden part thou shalt make me to know wisdom" (Psalm 51:5–6). We discussed the inherit Adamic nature of mankind and the blood of Jesus through salvation that makes us righteous. L. V.

confessed something was missing, and she knew she needed God in her life. Sin confession was made that night, and she accepted Christ in her heart. That following Sunday, she became a member of my church and worked with the children's Sunday School for years until she relocated to another state. I gave a short explanation on the verse: "And the peace of God, which passeth all understanding, shall keep your hearts and minds through Christ Jesus" (Philippians 4:7). Before lunch was over, she confessed her sins to Christ and according to Acts 3:19.

Nourishment for the Soul

- Using three Bible versions, study main scriptures and interpret them in your own words.
- Study and memorize one of the tracts "The Roman Road" or "The Four Spiritual Laws."

NOURISHMENT FOR THE SOUL

CHAPTER 3
Personalize

The soul winner's consultation must be made real to the patient's heart condition. The soul winner is the *Nurse* who prepares the patient and the atmosphere for an appointment with the Great Physician, Jesus Christ.

The soul winner is the Nurse who prepares the patient. The Nurse monitors vital signs and reviews the patient's admission paperwork. The Nurse assesses all subjective and objective information. The Nurse is responsible for gathering data on the patient's previous pain relief and treatment methods of the disorder, including prescribed and over-the-counter medications. The Nurse advises patients on preventative services, health screening, and present medication regimens. Also, the Nurse is responsible for providing information on the latest and best procedures for long-lasting results. Additionally, the Nurse must display soft skills at all times. This means the Clinician provides active listening, compassion, integrity, and diligence while preparing a tranquil environment and assurance of confidentiality.

The soul winner must create an atmosphere in which the patient understands that he is not alone. Sin is common to all of us (Romans 3:23).

PREPARE THE PATIENT

Show the patient that his well-being is your concern. Your patient does not care how much you know, but it is important that he knows how much you care.

- *Anesthesia.* Walk after the Spirit, not after the flesh. Be sure to yield to the control of the Holy Spirit. Be sure the word is in your heart and life.
- *Life Support.* Hide the word in your heart that you will not sin against God (Psalm 119:11). Be supportive! Remember you were once lost in sin and Jesus took you in. Let the patient know that you understand where he is. Tell him how God delivered you.
- *Bedside Manner.* Be optimistic. Regardless of the circumstances, believe in the Word and always glorify Jehovah God as the only true and living God—the source of hope, joy, and love.
- *Vital Signs.* Be a Good Samaritan. Never refuse an opportunity to help somebody in need of healing (from sin). Do not be so heavenly minded (pious) that you are no earthly good. Jesus the Christ was and is the perfect sacrifice for the sins of man. He was and is the perfect Lamb of God, without blemish and without sin. What can wash away our sins? Nothing but the blood of Jesus! When you share your conversion experience, you should *focus on the death, burial, and resurrection of Jesus Christ.* It is the salvation story (the story of Jesus Christ) that converts, convinces, convicts, and controls man's sinful nature (1 Corinthians 15:1–5; 2 Corinthians 5:17). Although you may have had a miraculous conversion or a profound testimony, neither can compare to Jesus's story. Always tell Jesus's story.

THE NURSE'S PERSONAL WITNESSING TOOLS (MEDICINE BAG)

Patience. The soul winner must remember how patient God was with him and show patience toward others (Romans 5:8).

Long-suffering. The soul winner must remember how long God dealt with him and tolerated his sinfulness. Do not be weary in well doing (Galatians 6:9).

Encouragement. The soul winner must remember that God is the God of hope. Glorify the name of Jesus before men and they will come to believe and trust in God (Matthew 5:16).

Love. The soul winner must remember God loves us unconditionally. We owe it to God to love our fellow man as we love ourselves. Always remind the patient of God's unconditional love (John 3:16–17).

THE PERSONAL CONSULTATION (EVALUATION)

> Meet the Patient on His Territory
>
> When the soul winner presents the Gospel well, the patient should feel that the message is just for him or her. Demonstrate your interest in his well-being. Let him know his well-being is your main concern. *Personalize* your presentation of the Gospel. Create an atmosphere in which the patient feels that he is not alone. Let him know that sin is a common disease that runs rampant among all mankind. Use yourself as an example. All of us have sinned and come short of the glory of God (Romans 3:23).

> Establish Common Ground with the Patient
>
> The soul winner must remember that he was once in sin and God delivered him. He cannot afford to be pious. The perfection of your walk is not the issue. The perfection of Jesus Christ is the issue.

> Check the Patient's Heartbeat

Make sure the patient clearly understands his condition and knows what it will take (the course of treatment) to heal his condition—his heartfelt convictions.

> Demonstrate Love for the Patient

Confirm God's love by your display of loving support. Exercise godly character—be a "living testimony." Avoid getting agitated or angry with the patient. Demonstrate tender heartedness and loving kindness. Remember, the patient is afraid and needs a lot of assurance and compassion. Confirm God's concern for the patient.

> Exemplify Your Love for God

Jesus Christ possesses a great passion for souls. The four Gospels (Matthew, Mark, Luke, and John) record brief accounts of Jesus's tireless grace, tender mercy, and loving compassion for people. Pastor Charles Stanley states: "We must possess a passion for God and a compassion for mankind, if we are going to reach the world for Christ." Jesus's heart went out to the lost and guilty sinners. He came to "seek and save" the lost (Luke 19:10). Such is the case with the soul winner. He or she must pray for passion and compassion and walk in the Spirit of the Almighty God.

SHARING THE GOSPEL WITH
NEIGHBORS IN THE CITY
Brian Bakke

Over the last 35 years, I have lived in two inner-city neighborhoods in Chicago and Washington, DC. My Chicago neighborhood is one of the most densely populated neighborhoods in the USA. It was a port of entry neighborhood for immigrants who spoke more than 100 languages and dialects. It was also a dumping ground for mentally ill people who were removed from the state-run mental hospitals and was the center for homeless people who lived in shelters or on the streets. The neighborhood had more senior adults living alone than any other part of Chicago and it was home to more than 25 rival street gangs, including two gangs that claimed the intersection where I lived for 15 years. My DC neighborhood was built by freed slaves after the Civil War. Years later, the neighborhood rivaled Harlem as the place to be if you were a poet, singer, musician, or writer. Most of the commercial district was burned down by rioters after Dr. Martin Luther King was assassinated. Two decades later, the neighborhood imploded due to the crack epidemic. Today, this area is one of the fastest gentrifying neighborhoods in the USA, moving from 96 percent Black when we moved in to about 30 percent Black, while whites now compose the majority. Most of the new residents are young adult white people who graduated from elite universities and graduate programs.

How does one share the Gospel in the city was made even more interesting when I put the question this way: How does a man who looks like a cop share Jesus with gang members who claim the neighborhood as their turf? How does an Evangelical share Jesus with his Muslim neighbors, gay and lesbian neighbors, or highly educated secular elites? How does a white man enter a historic Black neighborhood and share the Gospel with his Black neighbors? How does one share Jesus with people who grew up in homes where nobody goes to church or reads a Bible and denies the existence of God? For me, each of these people groups have been touched by my ability to be their neighbor and living a life that shows I care for them regardless of their belief, family history or current condition.

Luke 9:1–6 shows Jesus's ministry model of Mission in Reverse for such a neighborhood.

> When Jesus had called the Twelve together, he gave them power and authority to drive out all demons and to cure diseases, and he sent them out to proclaim the kingdom of God and to heal the sick. He told them: "Take nothing for the journey—no staff, no bag, no bread, no money, no extra shirt. Whatever house you enter, stay there until you leave that town. If people do not welcome you, leave their town and shake the dust off your feet as a testimony against them." So, they set out and went from village to village, proclaiming the good news and healing people everywhere. (NIV)

Two women who mentored me more than 35 years ago taught me my mission strategy which they called Mission in Reverse. These dear sisters read the Luke 9 text and told me, "Become a neighbor. Allow people to get to know you. Drop your agenda and your time schedule! Listen to the neighbors. Work to earn their trust. Do what your neighbors tell you. Then watch God work!" The Gospel of Luke chapter 9 demonstrates Mission in Reverse. Jesus sent them out with no weapons, food, money, or extra clothes. To me, this means that I do not carry a weapon (a staff was used for protection at that time), for I must trust God and my neighbors for my protection. "No bag or purse…" means to not have a bank account filled with money from outside interests into the hood. It also means I must trust in the generosity of new neighbors when I am in need. This will show my neighbors I need them more than they need me. "Stay there…" means living at the level of the people who were there when I arrived. This has meant a simple home and lifestyle. Jesus presents a paradox: He gave his followers tremendous power in the spiritual realm, and at the same time, he sent them out completely powerless in the physical realm. I believe Jesus did this so that his followers would be totally dependent on the people they were supposed to preach to and heal. If Jesus loaded his followers with gold, clothes, and gave them weapons or a group of armed men to protect them, the Disciples would be arrogant and ruin any opportunity to share the Good News. What happened was that after the long walk to the place Jesus sent them, his Disciples were tired, hungry, and smelled bad. They needed a bath, food, and a safe place to stay, but they didn't have money to pay for any of these things. Jesus's admonition to "stay in the first house that welcomes you" guaranteed they would be staying with the poor, because the door of the poor opens long before the door of the wealthy. Jesus did this because he knew the word would get out that these strangers had power to heal people and the rich would want to buy this power for themselves. God used these Disciples to live out their faith in front of others. And the people responded.

HOW TO PUT MISSION IN REVERSE INTO ACTION TODAY

My first apartment was on the border of two rival gang nations. There was a lot of violence in front of our apartment, but our phone went dead each time we called 911. After nine months of the phone going dead each time we called the police, I started walking into the gang fights. The young men would stop fighting and look at me. I would let them know the fight was over and they were free to go home. They would walk away from the fight, wondering aloud what just happened. I never grabbed or hit anyone, but walked out and declared peace for three years. Gang members got to know me. Finally, one gang leader asked me a profound question, "We love to play basketball. There is a church a couple blocks away that has a gym. If you get us in there, we will get off your corner. Can you do this for us?" I heard the voice of God through a gang leader and I obeyed. This is how the Miracle League got started. Each night, I would be in the front door of the church to greet each team and search them for weapons each time they came into the building. Each night, players would hear the rules, told to

"Respect the House," join in a Bible study, and hear the Gospel shared in a way they could hear it. After a couple of years, the gang members calmed down and began to trust me. Youth pastors and gang members told others about what was happening. The league stopped the shooting war in my neighborhood. After five years, the ministry went citywide. At its peak, there were more than 350 kids hearing and watching the Gospel being lived out by the coaches, referees, and the leaders of this ministry. Today, I have sons and grandsons in faith all over the city, who left the gangs and are now pastors because of their involvement in the Miracle League. Since that conversation with the gang leader, I have been given specific ministry directions by God speaking to me directly through a group of Korean-speaking senior adults, a former prostitute, young adult artists, a small group of irate old ladies, and even a drunken one-armed homeless man named Clarence, who cursed and swore at me as he gave me God's specific answer to a detailed prayer request that only my best friend and I knew about. Each time, I listened and obeyed. Each ministry started without any funding. Each time a ministry would get started, I would come to the point where I would call out to God and the Almighty would give me a gift: someone from the neighborhood who had been praying for the opportunity to help such a ministry.

My wife and I moved into a row house in Washington, DC, in 2001. We joined a local church and began to immerse ourselves in the African American community. We learned that church members commute into the city for church services every Sunday. There are dozens of other commuter congregations that meet within a short walk of our home. Mission in Reverse means I am incarnate not in a car. I asked God how to be a good neighbor in this context. God gave me a specific answer. "Buy a broom and use it. Clean until I tell you to stop. Do not speak until spoken to. Your neighbors will tell you what to do next." When I started sweeping, there were six drug houses on our street and a 24-hour drive-through drug market in each intersection. Drugs and weapons were stored in the alley behind our house. Each morning, I would clean the neighborhood and take everything I found and throw it away. I would sweep around the dealers as they tried to sell heroin. Each day, the dealers threatened me, but none ever attacked me. After a few months of sweeping, a woman told me she had been watching me and asked why I was cleaning the street. I told her I was being a neighbor and she thanked me. I thanked her and said it was an honor to be her neighbor. By the end of that week, neighbors were waving to me calling me by name. Not too long afterward, the grandmothers on the block invited me into an important conversation, "We have been trying to get the city to put in speed humps on our street. Cars race up and down the street and hit our kids." I was asked to circulate a petition asking the city to install the speed humps. A month later, a crew put the speed humps in. The speed and volume on our block went way down. One day, thieves tried to break into our home over the course of a weekend while we were away. We learned our neighbors got involved and called the police repeatedly. We invited the neighbors that got involved over for supper. We shared stories until the early morning. Then we gave the key to our house and car and the house security code to each of our neighbors. We told them if they cared enough to get involved in such a way, we wanted them to know that we trusted them. Since then, all of us have become good friends.

That evening led to another conversation with neighbors who asked me to help them replant the trees on our block that were cut down during the crack wars. We have planted all the new trees on the block, and I asked neighbors to give money to help cover the cost of the trees. In each case, our neighbors gave too much money, so I had to tell them to stop. One day, a neighbor stopped me on the sidewalk and said, "There is a lot of spiritual warfare here. We need to gather together on a regular basis and pray for the neighborhood." So a prayer group started meeting in our home. I now get into conversations with my secular neighbors about justice, safety, gentrification, city services, and the quality of life. When my neighbors ask me why I am so involved in these things, I share my testimony and faith in Jesus. Each day when I go out with my broom, I clean 10 city blocks and pick up dog mess, food, dead rats, credit cards and driver's licenses, and even weapons. While cleaning, I ask God to bless the neighborhood with peace, grace, safety, and joy. My sweeping times have become known by neighbors who come looking for me, knowing I will stop and listen to them.

After renting our row house for seven years, we bought it. Shortly after we bought it, we started the process of repairing it. We tore the face of the house off before it fell off into the street. Then we asked neighbors to give us advice on the extensive structural damage throughout; they told us what to do. We said we would follow their advice. We tore down the house from the roof to the subfloor, from the interior of the new front face all the way to the back alley. Neighbors helped us move our things into storage and gave tools, hundreds of hours of construction help, food, and water as we rebuilt our place. Five men on our block who work in construction taught me how to rebuild the house. Neighbors told us that they were helping us because they loved us and that they did not want to see us leave the block. Hour after hour, I would be working with a Muslim man. And for even longer amounts of time, I would work side by side with a gay man. In each case, we built trust by listening to each other and not being offended by what the other said. And they would ask me about my faith.

We have the names, cell phone numbers, and emails of the people that live on our street. When I leave for a trip, our neighbors care for my wife and our house. If both of us leave, a neighbor moves our car so we do not get street cleaning tickets. Another collects our mail and comes in and turns on different lights and walks through to make sure the house is okay. Once when I was on a trip, my wife needed to go the hospital. Neighbors took her to the emergency room and waited with her until she was admitted. Then another neighbor came into our house and packed a bag with food and her clothes. Neighbors gave her a ride back to our home. When I get back from a trip, I share a short story about two or three churches in another city doing beautiful things with street kids or trafficked women or about work in the prisons. After reading my reflection, they come to me with new questions.

Over the past 15 years, I have swept the sidewalks and cleaned the gutters in front of a Mosque one block south of our home. Each time I sweep in front of the Mosque, I pray that God would bless the community of the Mosque with love, grace, peace, and safety. I learned a group of white supremacists planned to attack the Mosque on the 20th anniversary of the Million Man March. I was in front of the Mosque that day praying and sweeping. Men from the Mosque asked me what I was doing because I was out in front of the Mosque for hours. I told them I knew about the threat against them, and if the white terrorists came to attack the Mosque, they will have to kill me first. One of the men asked me if I had a gun. I told them I have never had a gun and don't need one. All that day, men from the Mosque hugged me and thanked me for standing with them that day. The white terrorists never came, but my actions led the Imam to invite me to share my testimony with the Mosque's Board of Directors. The Imam started the meeting, "I have asked Brian to share his testimony and how he is a neighbor on this street. I think his story is interesting and maybe we can ask him questions about why he does what he does on this street. I think we can learn from him and his witness." I shared some of the things that happened with our neighbors over the years. My sharing and the question-and-answer sessions lasted for two hours. I walked home from this meeting wearing a suit. Neighbors were out working in their gardens. They asked me why I was dressed so nicely. I told them I had a meeting at the Mosque. My neighbors asked what we talked about. It took me an hour to walk one block home because so many neighbors asked about my suit and the meeting with the leaders of the Mosque. Last summer, the Imam invited me to attend an event which would build unity, trust, and respect among Jews, Muslims, and Christians. When I entered the Mosque, I learned the ceremony was being broadcast on live Global TV. The Imam asked the General Secretary of the world's largest Muslim organization, the Secretary General of the World Evangelical Alliance, and a powerful Rabbi to come to the front of the room and join him at the podium. The Imam asked each of these three men to talk about acts of unity, trust, and respect among Jews, Muslims, and Christians. Then the Imam looked into the TV camera and said, "There is a young man here who is an Evangelical Christian, his name is Brian Bakke. He put his life in harm's way when our Mosque was under threat; Brian put his life on the line for us. He is an example of what we hope to achieve with the signing of this document." I had no idea he would say anything about something that happened many years ago. The leaders in the room came to speak with me. Each of them asked me why I would do what I did. I told all of them the same thing, "I was just being a neighbor."

EVANGELISM FROM A THEATRICAL ARTS PERSPECTIVE POSITIVE PERSPECTIVE MENTORS AND EDUCATIONAL SERVICES
Willie A. Taylor

Evangelism means preaching, announcing, or otherwise communicating the gospel message that Jesus Christ is not only the Son of God, but also gave His life as a sacrifice for our sins. https://www.christianity.com/wiki/christian-terms/what-is-evangelism.html

Theatrical Arts is a collaborative form of expression and communication that uses live performers to present the experience of a real or imagined event before a live audience in a specific place. https://en.wikipedia.org/wiki/Theatre

Theatrical Evangelism is the act of communicating the gospel message using live performers at live events or on digital platforms.

Theatrical Evangelism is focused on four groups of people:

- ✓ Those who have not heard the Gospel of Christ
- ✓ Those who do not understand the Gospel of Christ
- ✓ Those who have not yet accepted the Gospel of Christ
- ✓ Those who need to strengthen or reaffirm belief in the Gospel of Christ

There is a great need for theatrical arts as a tool in evangelism. In today's climate, people are greatly influenced by what they see and hear on TV, radio, and the various social media platforms. They make life-changing decisions based on the images and messages that shape their thinking and control their actions. We already know that the Gospel has the power to make a dramatic impact in the lives of people, so it's imperative that we engage theatrical arts as a method to share the gospel good news and not leave this medium with inadequate Christian participation. We need to compete in this arena to counter secular impact so that the "gates of hell shall not prevail" (Matthew 16:18). Evangelism through theatrical arts is a battlefield on which the church should resist and rebel against false teachings and lifestyles that lead people down the wrong paths. It can instruct and correct people to believe in the Word and adjust their lives to conform to the will of God when it is consistent with and does not contradict the teachings of the Bible.

God's Word calls us to "always be prepared to give an answer to everyone who asks you to give the reason for the hope that you have" (1 Peter 3:15).

If evangelism is meant to communicate the gospel message, theatrical arts must be given serious consideration. The gospel needs to be explained as well as proclaimed. Bearing in mind how people process information, the most widely accepted model of learning styles is called the VARK model which suggests that visual learners learn best by seeing, auditory learners learn best by hearing, reading/writing learners learn best by reading and writing, and kinesthetic (physical) learners learn best by moving and doing.

https://harappa.education/harappa-diaries/vark-learning-style/

Theatrical arts incorporate all of these learning styles and, therefore, is extremely appropriate for a diverse audience to receive the gospel message.

Drama can be a very powerful tool to lead people to Christ, to convey God's messages and teach His principles in a fun way that appeals to all ages. With the technological advances of our society, people are accustomed to being entertained. They crave new and exciting experiences; therefore, even unbelievers are receptive to Christian drama, making it a powerful evangelism tool. Drama is an under-used essential means of showcasing the gospel on stage for people to see and hear.

Proverbs 29:18 says that where there is no vision, the people perish. Theatrical arts in evangelism can be likened to biblical scenarios in which communications through dreams and visions give instructions and directions for people to follow in order for the will of God to be manifested in their lives and for the good of others.

Matthew 1:20–24 details how Joseph, Mary's fiancé, saw and heard an angel declare in a dream confirmation that he should marry her and affirmation of the truth of her conception. This scenario can be performed to emphasize the truth about the virgin birth and show a man struggling with what he thought were the only two options of having Mary stoned or breaking the engagement. It can show the wisdom in allowing God's guidance for the situation.

Acts 9–11 shares the visions God gave to Ananias, Cornelius, and Peter which prepared them to receive Saul after his conversion on the Damascus Road. It can be used to combat the biases we have toward people who come into the faith, but are widely known for their wicked past.

I have used theatrical arts as an evangelism tool on many occasions. One, entitled "Breakout" is based on Romans 7:14–25 (see script below). It is a fluid ever-changing drama that encourages audience participation in the evangelical process by responding to the needs and request for direction from the main character. Although the dialog requires the main character to ad lib, as it can be different from audience to audience, it still centers around the sinful nature of man and our need to believe and receive Jesus Christ who will set us free from the clutches of the evil one.

This theatrical presentation was initially created to encourage and provoke men to escape those things in their lives that prevent them from fully embracing God's forgiveness and living free as a result of the debt of sin fully paid by Jesus Christ. It has been used at youth retreats to show young people the dangers of drugs and alcohol abuse. It has been performed at Good Friday and Easter services to illustrate the depravity of mankind when we live outside of relationship with God and, how the finished work that Christ did on the cross paid the penalty for our sins and redeemed us back to God. "Breakout is a one-man monologue depicting how sin shackles men and causes us to do things that we know are wrong but can't seem to get out of the cycle of behaviors that keeps us bound. Sin is represented in the drama by heavy chains that physically bind the man. In the beginning, it depicts how the power of sin can cause us to rebel and try to live our lives independently of God" (v. 14–21). The drama reveals many of the sinful actions and thoughts that dominate our daily existence. At the same time, it portrays the anguish of being unable to correct what we know is self-destructive behavior. Next, it illustrates how the Word of God and heeding wise counsel can be instrumental in our deliverance and freedom to live as God purposed us (v. 21–24). A vivid picture of the man struggling to be free as a result of newfound strength and determination is shown through his physical effort to become free of the chains that bind him. In his fight to be free, he quotes scripture and praises God even when he is not yet completely free. It concludes with the man being loosed from his chains and showing thankfulness, praise, and gratitude to God. His declaration is to live according to God's plan.

"Breakout" is effective because men can see the reality of their lives reflected through drama rather than hearing about it from a counselor. God used art to show me my own life and my need for Him. I began to use art to share the gospel with others in the same way it had been used with me.

In conclusion, implementing theatrical arts as a vehicle to enhance evangelism is necessary. Not only does it cover all of the basic methods people use to learn, but it is also a medium that can have a longer lasting impact on the viewer. Just as you remember what happened in your favorite movie years after your first viewing, the Christian messages delivered by theatrical arts will remain imbedded in the minds and hearts of those who are spectators. As the seeds are planted and watered, eventually, they will become believers in the gospel message.

BREAKOUT PICTORIAL (10-12-2019 PERFORMANCE)

Each dialogue is adapted in each performance for the particular audience or occasion.

Breakout Photos

INCARNATIONAL EVANGELISM
Bryan McCabe

One of the most effective tools in reaching people with the good news of the gospel of Jesus Christ is incarnational evangelism. John 1:14 says, "And the Word became flesh and dwelt among us, and we have seen his glory, glory as of the only Son from the Father, full of grace and truth." That means that God entered into the human condition, becoming present with us during his mission of living a perfect life. He suffered and died on the cross, was raised to life, and interacted with many people before ascending to heaven. Jesus said "Follow Me" more than 30 times in scripture, and if our goal, as Christians, if to follow Jesus, then it makes sense that we should be present with people, just as Jesus modeled for us, in our evangelism. Incarnational Evangelism involves pursuing shared experiences, hopes, and circumstances with people, as opposed to simply sharing information about God without building a relationship.

The concept sounds so simple, but many Christians struggle to live out an incarnational approach. Relationships are messy. It might seem easier or more transactional to simply tell people about Jesus from afar. It's true that people do come to Christ through things like large events or through televangelists, methodologies that are not inherently incarnational. Many modern people, though, are growing increasingly skeptical of Christianity. People may be interested in learning more about Jesus, but they are often wary of Christianity, due to interactions with hypocritical Christians. These are Christians whose lifestyles are contrary to Jesus's message. Many times, Christians are overly judgmental and divisive over ideologies. More and more people who are far from God or seeking to learn more about God are looking for authenticity through meaningful relationships lived out in practical ways.

An incarnational approach to evangelism leads to a healthy process of being able to contextualize the gospel. While God never changes, there are many different cultures and worldviews within those cultures. In the book *Justice, Mercy, and Humility,* Peter Kuzmic notes that "Entering the context is of crucial importance. Jesus did not pick up a heavenly megaphone to shout down to the inhabitants of Planet Earth: 'Repent!' He entered human history and human flesh. He was hungry. He was thirsty. He became a refugee. Contextualization is not just knowledge of the other context, but being willing to identify yourself with the context and become vulnerable" (p. 157). Just like Jesus spent time with people, listening and learning, and in general, being present, so, too, should we take the time to get to know people by spending time with them where they live, work, and play.

In his letter to the Philippians, the Apostle Paul encourages the church to model their lives after Christ Jesus, "who, though he was in the form of God, did not count equality with God a thing to be grasped, but emptied himself, by taking the form of a servant, being born in the likeness of men. And being found in human form, he humbled himself by becoming obedient to the point of death, even death on a cross. Therefore, God has highly exalted him and bestowed on him the name that is above every name, so that at the name of Jesus every knee should bow, in heaven and on earth and under the earth, and every tongue confess that Jesus Christ is Lord, to the glory of God the Father" (Philippians 2:6–11). The goal with Incarnational Evangelism is to serve others in order to bring honor and glory to God. We roll up our sleeves and get into the messiness in the trenches of people's lives. And as we serve them there, with actions and words, we bear witness to God's transforming work in the world and in individual lives.

Kris Rocke and Joel Van Dyke share in *Geography of Grace* that "the incarnation is not merely a doctrine disconnected from street reality, rather it has profound implications for day-to-day life and ministry. At the risk of reducing the incarnation to a formula, we might think about it in three ways: *God in Christ, Christ in us, Us in the world.* We exist to point to, lift up, and celebrate the Incarnate Christ. We need to learn to hit the streets with the poetic license found in Ephesians 2:10. This calls for a radical presence" (p. 73). The concept of radical presence really captures the essence of Incarnational Evangelism well. We choose to be fully present with our family, friends, coworkers, and neighbors. And we especially choose to be radically present with people on the margins of society, including orphans, widows, refugees, and people experiencing poverty. "For we are his workmanship, created in Christ Jesus for good works, which God prepared beforehand, that we should walk in them" (Ephesians 2:10).

Incarnational Evangelism means that we are truly with people, physically present with them and also emotionally, mentally, and spiritually present with them. That can be hard to do in a society that has many barriers that keep people divided, and also many things that grab our attention to the point where we can be physically present with people without giving our full attention. Rocke and Van Dyke suggest that the best "prepositional option for the mission of the church is *"with."* This is the incarnational preposition—*Immanuel* (God with us). When this preposition drives the mission, whether it's the church, organization, or even a short-term mission project, the potential to transform *both* the leaders *and* the people they seek to serve is heightened. Along with potential there is cost—these ministries require a much higher investment of time and relational energy (though much more is released in the long run)" (p. 75). Incarnational Evangelism may seem inefficient and time-consuming, but the lasting positive outcomes of the approach are well worth it.

What does Incarnational Evangelism look like, practically speaking? As a pastor and a leader in my city, the journey of Incarnational Evangelism has been a path filled with trial and error. While there are challenges, the approach can be extremely effective. In 2006, I helped to start up a youth mentoring program called LAMP (Learning and Mentoring Partnership) with members of my church, North Way Christian Community, in the city of Pittsburgh, Pennsylvania. We matched up volunteer mentors from our church in one-to-one relationships with children living in an underserved urban neighborhood called Homewood. The mentors committed to building a relationship with a mentee for at least a one-year commitment, visiting with their mentee for several hours once a week. At the end of the yearlong commitment, nearly all of the mentors committed to signing up for another year. Many of the mentoring matches have endured all of the way through when children graduate from high school, and today, as adults, the mentoring relationships have turned into lifelong friendships. Many children in the mentoring relationships have become followers of Jesus through the relational, incarnational approach of the mentors from the church. Where geographical and socioeconomic barriers might previously have separated church members from building meaningful relationships with marginalized children in Homewood, an incarnational approach through mentoring relationships brought people together, all for the sake of bringing glory to God.

As the LAMP mentoring program gained momentum, I was helping to lead the way in making mentoring matches and building relationships with kids and families in Homewood who we could match up with mentors from the church. I was matched in a mentoring relationship early on, so I did have the opportunity to be relationally invested and present with a young person in the neighborhood. However, I was living with my family about 30 minutes away from Homewood. I was not as effective as I could have been in trying to lead LAMP living so far away, and my family was relatively disconnected from my ministry with families in Homewood. So my wife and I made the decision to move our family to Homewood. We bought a house right next to the elementary school where we were making most of the LAMP mentoring matches. Over the course of time, we began to open our home up to our neighbors in Homewood. We started throwing block parties. We initiated a community meal every Monday night where we would prepare a meal and open up our table to anyone who wanted to join. My kids hung out with kids from the neighborhood. We had lots of people who visited with us over the years. Sometimes, we struggled with establishing boundaries, so there were at times struggles with being overly engaged relationally. We learned some family rhythms over time that helped with that. Our goal was to simply be radically present with people and to share our lives with others in order to point people to God and model what a relationship with Jesus is like. It has been a great privilege to walk alongside people relationally and see them grow in their relationship with God. We were there to pray with people, to grieve with people, to celebrate with people, and to walk alongside of people as they sought to follow Jesus. There was tremendous heartbreak when young people were incarcerated or killed by gun violence. But there was much more tremendous celebration and breakthrough that we experienced with our neighbors in Homewood over time. It's truly a privilege to walk alongside of people for years and see God at work in their lives.

Incarnational Evangelism is transformational for the follower of Jesus who is sharing their faith and their life, and it is transformational for the person who may be seeking to discover more about God. Radical presence may involve building a youth mentoring relationship or moving a family into a neighborhood where the Lord is calling. It can look like much, much more though. Radical presence can take place with the powerful and the powerless. Christians are needed to be radically present in the board rooms of corporations, in the halls of power in government, and in culture shaping industries like media or professional sports. I have a good friend who serves as a chaplain to one of Pittsburgh's professional sports teams. His main goal, along with his wife, is to be radically present with people on the team and with their families in order to help to orient their lives in God's Story. He spends a tremendous amount of time building meaningful relationships and helping people to navigate through the ups and downs of professional sports and the tremendous platform that comes with that line of work. I have another friend who leads the K-12 education system for an entire country. By spending significant amounts of time in underperforming schools in the country, he has been able to introduce transformational strategies that have made a significant positive impact in the lives of hundreds of thousands of children, all as an extension of his Christian faith and his commitment to radical presence with people. What I love about him is also that he is a pastor and an evangelist. When he's not working as an educational leader, you'll often find him being radically present with people, going into marginalized neighborhoods with members of his church, and sharing the love of Christ with vulnerable people in his city.

More recently, our church in Pittsburgh has established a ministry hub in another urban neighborhood. We're reaching people with the good news of the Gospel of Jesus Christ, and it's happening with an intentional, incarnational approach. Our goal is to build relationships with people for many years to come. There will be opportunities to share the gospel with words, and we will often share the gospel through actions, as well. Through after-school programs for young people, ministry opportunities with older adults, social entrepreneurship opportunities, and initiatives around things like food, housing, refugee care, and serving families who have been impacted by incarceration, the ministry hub is a place where radical presence and Incarnational Evangelism point people toward a life-changing relationship with Jesus. I'm excited to see what God is going to do through the ministry hub in the coming years as our church continues to experiment with approaches to incarnational evangelism. There will be failures and there will be challenges, but we are fully empowered by God to overcome any barriers and the authentic relationships are definitely worth it!

Incarnational Evangelism is not the only approach to evangelism. God works through many different ways to accomplish his redemptive mission in this world. However, taking an incarnational approach by being radically present with people where they live, work, and play, can yield amazing results. As Christians, the light of Christ shines through us as we build meaningful relationships with others. "Therefore, as you received Christ Jesus the Lord, so walk in him, rooted and built up in him and established in the faith, just as you were taught, abounding in thanksgiving" (Colossians 2:6). In an increasingly skeptical world that is overloaded with information and ideologies, Incarnational Evangelism can be an effective way of cutting through all of the noise and pointing people to the hope that is found in Christ.

EVANGELISM THROUGH GRIEF
Arletha Orr

Often times in life, we as women neglect ourselves to take care of others around us. We put our dreams and goals on hold to help others such as our significant other, children and/or family, achieve their goals. By the time we've helped everyone else, we're too exhausted to do what we want to do. We're tired and burnt out from being the wife, mom, teacher, caregiver, lover, friend, therapist, nurse, just to name a few. When do we accomplish what we want to do in life? When do we revisit our dreams and goals—and live for us?

If you are a woman, I'm pretty sure you have felt that way at least once in your life. Most of the time, we do forget ourselves and focus on others, but here's the killer part, we never notice it until years have passed and then we find that it's too late.

In July 2008, I birthed my first child; she was my world. I was a single parent, so we spent a lot of time together. I had begun to instill in her morals and values to prepare her for life (they're never too young). I made sure she started school at the appropriate age so that she could start learning to be interactive with other kids, learn motor skills, and more. She knew how to act at church and even at restaurants. Ha! I'll never forget it, I got accepted into nursing school, but I had to quit because I couldn't focus like I needed to. I wanted to make sure she had everything she needed, so I resigned from nursing school and chose something a little less complicated that didn't require so much of my time.

For five years, it was just the two of us. In May 2012, I met my husband, and in May 2013, we were married. It was a joy to have him around to have a father figure in my baby's life and also to have a man around the house. During this time, he taught our daughter how to ride her bike, rake leaves, assisted with homework, and so much more. We were both "happy as hyenas."

In December 2014, God blessed us with the addition of a boy child to our family. We were all excited! I had the opportunity to birth my second child, a son. It was my husband's first son and my daughter had the adventure of being a big sister. They loved each other. They were both enrolled in school and doing great. We attended church as a family. We went on vacations and so much more. Life was perfect! It was the absolute best eight years of my life!

In May 2016, I lost it all. My hubby picked up the babies from after school care, and as they were traveling home, they were struck by an Amtrak train. No one in my family survived! I had recently spoken with my husband an hour before the accident occurred. It's amazing how one day everything can be perfect, but within the next second, it all vanishes. That day was no different than any other. Normal drop off, work and school day, but that evening changed my life.

During this time of grief, unbeknown to me, I had lost or hidden some things that made me happy, and also, I had built resentment in my heart against God. Our goal as a mom and wife is to make sure that everyone is taken care of in the house and that's exactly what we do but we neglect ourselves. Please don't misunderstand me here. Being a wife and mom were the *best* things that ever happened to me in my life, but during that time, we should never forget or lose focus on ourselves. Why would God allow this to happen to me? I was and currently a faithful churchgoer, lived by the Word of God, and a faithful tithe payer. This can't be happening to me. I don't deserve this.

I was devastated! I was broken! I was empty! I was lost! I literally felt as if I was in a pit because I felt as if I had nothing. I felt isolated, hurt, and all the above. My family was my everything. I loved being a mom and a wife.

At that moment, I did what I knew to do, and that was to pray. Psalm 34:18 MSG says, "If your heart is broken, you'll find God right there; if you're kicked in the gut, he'll help you catch your breath." God came and spoke one word, and it changed my entire life: "Live!"

Matthew 5:4 MSG states, "You're blessed when you feel you've lost what is most dear to you. Only then can you be embraced by the

One most dear to you." Just as I thought my world had turned upside down, the Holy Spirit was my comforter to lead and guide me through grief.

Life happens. What do you have to hold on to when you're going through? That was the toughest moment I've ever had to experience in life, but I know I had God to lead and guide me through, and He did. He has restored my joy! He has restored my peace! He has revealed so much about me to me, and I thank Him for it.

I want to encourage you to come out of that dry place. The joy of the Lord is your strength (Nehemiah 8:10 NKJV). Whatever has you bound, let God free you from it so that you can be restored! Let God restore your joy! Let God restore your peace! Let God restore your mind. You deserve to accomplish what you want in life! You deserve everything you desire to have!

Rise up and take what's rightfully yours. You got this! You are more than a conqueror! You shall *live* and not die, and declare the works of the Lord! *Live*!

A SUICIDAL PERSON
Marchelle D. Lee

This type of person often requires professional counselors or persons trained to intervene in a potential suicidal crisis. Bloody, yelling, and screaming in pain, Ms. C. M. was being rolled down the hallway of our unit. There were many suicidal individuals that were admitted to our trauma unit during our tenure at the hospital. These persons had multiple spiritual heart dysfunctions along with a combination of the two that we discussed, especially Spiritual CHF. Their condition causes them to become easily fatigued, short-winded, desiring to give up on living earlier than most people. They need prodigious assistance to take each step daily. Others become their emotional oxygen, walker, and/or wheelchair long before their physical person starts to decline. Unless qualified and truly an expert, one needs to proceed with great thoughtfulness and care with persons deemed to be suicidal. The priority is to make sure they are safe from physical harm first. Then make sure back-up is near or on the way. Remember, the suicidal person feels no value, love, or hope; therefore, all conversations must lead to their value and a reason for living.

Ms. C. M. was known to be a very beautiful young woman. Yet that night, she was barely recognizable. She had been beaten by a dope dealer for lack of her boyfriend's payment for drugs. This young woman had bruises from the top of her head to her toes. She cried half the shift in excruciating pain for hours until staff could get it under control. Prior to being discharged from the hospital, without reservation, I knew she needed God in the worst way. She was scared to live and wanted to die. She talked about committing suicide and being afraid of her boyfriend and the dope dealer that had her beaten. She denied having any family that she could call or go home to. She felt unloved and devalued because she had been raped before she was beaten and brought to the hospital.

During her hospital stay, doctors talked to her about her near-death experience, a social worker came to talk about the need to find a safe place for herself. The chaplain came and prayed with her. The police came to question her, and as bad as she was beaten, she would not give up the names of the persons that assaulted her. Two days before her discharge, while she was walking in the cafeteria. I asked if I could speak with her. I explained that God loved her and had a plan and a purpose for her life. Scripture references were, "Cast your burden on the Lord, and he will sustain you; he will never permit the righteous to be moved" (Psalm 55:22). "For I know the thoughts that I think toward you, saith the LORD, thoughts of peace, and not of evil, to give you an expected end" (Jeremiah 29:11). We prayed and reviewed a few scriptures that evening, C. M. broke down crying, saying, "I know my life can be better than this." We talked about John 3:16–17, I shared my testimony with her and invited her to accept Jesus as her personal Lord and Savior and she did. The timing was right for Invitational Evangelism, which is usually on the spot and can occur in private or public. More often seen when the preacher gives the call to discipleship during a worship service.

NOURISHMENT FOR THE SOUL

Using Psalms 51, write an 8–10 line prayer of repentance.

NOURISHMENT FOR THE SOUL

CHAPTER 4
Picturize

The soul winner must paint a description of hope in the mind of the patient.

The soul winner is a *Therapist* who advises the patient of his condition and encourages him during rehabilitation, monitors the patient's progress, and assists the patient in following the Great Physician's orders for complete restoration and recovery.

THERAPEUTIC PICTURIZATION

Create Mental Pictures for Your Patient

Paint real pictures of life after death—Heaven and Hell. Emphasize eternal life in the presence of God (Heaven) and eternal separation in the absence of God (Hell). Heaven is the better choice. Heaven's eternal beauty, glory, and pleasure should utterly outweigh hell's gloom and doom.

Heaven. In the presence of Jesus, there is complete peace. Heaven is a prepared place for a prepared people. It is absence of pain and suffering. It is a land where the inhabitants (Christians) never grow old. It is a mansion where there is fullness of joy in the presence of Jesus, the Light of the World for all eternity.

Hell. In the absence of God, there is torment, anguish, and eternal damnation. Imagine being locked away in an asylum populated with insane people who are tormented day in and day out by their own insanity, despair, and hopelessness. That is hell! Imagine wanting to commit suicide in order to find relief from a pit of darkness and being unable to attain any kind of relief. That is hell! Imagine being separated from God for all eternity. That is hell.

Discussion. At this point, the facilitator generates a class discussion around what it is like to be separated from God. Read Matthew 26:36–46. For the first time, God the Father and Jesus the Son would be separated from each other. Jesus was not agonizing over dying for the sins of the world. What does Jesus mean when he pleads to God the Father to remove "the bitter cup"? How does Jesus's predicament in the Garden of Gethsemane compare to eternal separation from God?

Emphasize the Positive

Keep your comments cheerful and productive. Avoid aggressive confrontations. A quiet one-on-one conversation usually has better success.

Communicate Clearly

Make sure the patient clearly understands. Even though you may have to restate your message several times and in several ways, your message should be delivered consistently. Make your message clear and meaningful to the patient. Elaborate on the Word of God. Speak passionately and sincerely. Trust God for a miraculous healing and salvation.

Relate the Accurate and Relevant Truth

Employ examples to which the patient can relate. Tell biblical stories that relate to the patient's situation. All examples, demonstrations, and illustrations should be biblically supported. Always minister "Truth"— God's Word. Base your message on "the truth"—God's Word. Always present biblical stories and examples that are relevant to your patient's condition.

Pray for Guidance

Stay in constant communication with God through prayer. This is God's work. God alone reserves the right to conduct His work. Follow God's lead during the course of the operational procedure (soul winning). Acceptance or rejection of Jesus Christ is a life and death decision.

Communicate Hope. Exemplify Love

Regardless of the past or present, there is hope and God still loves. The patient should be challenged to a victorious present and a rewarding future.

Captivate Their Minds

Aim at the patient's heart while exemplifying hope and love. Treat the patient like you want to be treated. The patient will know you are a Christian by the love you show toward him. Regardless of the patient's past history, let him know there is hope for healing (from sin) in Jesus. Once saved, he can never be separated from the love of Jesus.

Appeal to the Patient's Ears and Eyes

Appeal to the patient's vision (eyes). Help the patient "see" what you mean. Most people learn best with visuals. Utilize visual aids such as tracts, videotapes, and Bible verses. Appeal to the patient's sense of hearing (ears). Actively listen and rephrase your message as needed to ensure the patient understands clearly.

EVANGELISM FROM THE URBAN PERSPECTIVE
Stephen C. White

And Jesus came and spoke to them, saying, "All authority has been given to Me in heaven and on earth. Go therefore and make disciples of all the nations, baptizing them in the name of the Father and of the Son and of the Holy Spirit, teaching them to observe all things that I have commanded you; and lo, I am with you always, even to the end of the age." Amen.
—Matthew 28:18–20

The church culture today is much different than past decades as we see numbers declining and communities suffering spiritual poverty. Thriving urban communities do not see the need for churches and are buying buildings that once housed worshiping communities and transforming them into lounges, clubs, food establishments, and other profiting institutions. The influence of the church community has lessened over the years due to a lack of evangelism and participation from those living in the area.

The Great Commission of Jesus Christ was given to His disciples and continues to this day. If men, women, boys, and girls are to know, experience, and have the love of the Father, evangelism must be a priority for the church and those who make up the church. In most communities across the country, urban communities are transitioning once again due to re-gentrification. Poor areas of cities are experiencing an influx of middle class and wealthy people who are renovating and rebuilding homes and businesses as they dislocate families of lesser financial means. If there ever was a time for urban evangelism, that time is now as people are struggling to belong somewhere and with someone.

Urban evangelism traces back to the instructions of Jesus as He informed His disciples that "You shall receive power when the Holy Spirit has come upon you; and you shall be witnesses to Me in Jerusalem, and in all Judea and Samaria, and to the end of the earth" (Acts 1:8). Jerusalem was the Urban area where many people lived, worked, and worshipped. It represented what we would call the urban community today filled with people of all walks of life. Business professionals, students, families, and those less fortunate than others who need to know that the God they cannot see does exist and Jesus is Lord!

To evangelize from the urban perspective is to live the gospel in the presence of those within the community. It means to "let your light so shine before men, that they see our good works and glorify our Father in heaven" (Matthew 5:16). Thomas Aquinas said, "Preach! And if you must, use words!" Believers of Jesus Christ and the church must be substance and evidence in order for nonbelievers will put their confidence in a God they cannot see. Yes, we must tell the urban communities about Jesus, who died, was buried, rose on the third day, ascended into heaven, and will come back to receive His church. In telling of this account, we must also demonstrate through lifestyle evangelism our confidence in the God they cannot see. The preached word must be followed by the lived word once the benediction is given or the account is shared. The saying "Action speaks louder than words" is an accurate statement and evangelism without action will not expand the kingdom of God.

Urban evangelism requires workers who see that "the harvest truly is plentiful, but the laborers are few. Therefore, pray the Lord of the harvest to send out laborers into His harvest" (Matthew 9:37–38). We need those who will pray and those who will be the answer to the prayers prayed. Many people in urban communities do not attend church simply because no one has ever asked them. As we become credible witnesses by being empowered by the Holy Spirit to represent Jesus to those who are lost, the urban community might pay attention and join us in a worship service.

It is true that the church is competing with the world to gain the attention of those living in the community, so we must be distinctively different from the world so others will want to follow us to church and accept our Lord and Savior Jesus Christ. Evangelism is simple when we trust God, obey God, and live for God in such a way that others will desire the God they cannot see because they see the fruit of the Spirit manifesting in us as we engage with them. Even though evangelism is simple, it is not easy. We have to do as Jesus instructed us: to deny ourselves, take up our cross, and follow Him. We must be constantly living our faith all the time, every time, until the end of time. There are no time outs or vacation breaks. We must be ambassadors of Christ continuously so those in urban communities will want to follow us as we follow Christ.

CROSS-CULTURAL EVANGELISM
Michael J. Mercurio

Introduction

At the very end of the Bible, God gives us a glimpse of heaven and the eternal reward that awaits his children. John, the Apostle, writes, "I looked and there before me was a great multitude that no one could count, from every nation, tribe, people and language, standing before the throne and in front of the Lamb" (Revelation 7:9).

The worshippers in this picture are very different from one another and yet they are all together. They are all together in one place, but they are probably also together with one heart. On earth, differences often cause division, but in the presence of God, we cannot love him unless we love each other. In one of his letters, John made this clear. "If anyone says, 'I love God,' yet hates his brother, he is a liar. For anyone who does not love his brother, whom he has seen, cannot love God, whom he has not seen" (1 John 4:20).

Practically speaking, if life in heaven is going to be filled with such love and togetherness, it only makes sense that every serious Christian should pray for and live out God's will—on earth as it is in heaven (Matthew 6:10). When this takes place, we get to demonstrate the reality of Jesus in our lives. We get to shine his light in a world of darkness, and we get to become his witnesses. In one of the last prayers that Jesus prayed, he spoke to the Father about us. "I pray…that all of them may be one, Father, just as you are in me, and I am in you. May they also be in us so that the world may believe that you have sent me" (John 17:20–21).

To practice unity in the midst of diversity and in a way that brings glory to Jesus is called "Cross-Cultural Evangelism."

THE NEED FOR CROSS-CULTURAL EVANGELISM

We live in the 21st century, but division and polarization still exist. Some might even say that they exist now in ways that it has never existed before. People are divided racially, economically, socially, and politically. Cable news, talk radio, and social media tend to push people into opposing camps. How can we ever come together?

The Good News of the Gospel is that, in Christ, we are united by his Holy Spirit and brought together in the name of our Heavenly Father. As the church, as people who are humbled by our common need for salvation and our utter inability to provide this for ourselves, we have a story to tell about what God has done. This story needs to be communicated first by the way that we live out our faith and love one another. Then, we can explain with words what people see in us.

Historically, the church has not done a very good job illustrating the kind of unity that we will one day experience in heaven. It has often been said that the 11:00 worship service on Sunday morning is the most segregated hour in America. So the need is first and foremost for the church to minister to itself and ask God to show us how to fulfill the heart of Jesus's prayer for oneness.

AN UNFOLDING STORY

My own journey is a long one, but here is a snapshot of what God has been doing lately. Currently, I am the lead pastor of a multi-cultural church in the suburbs of Washington, D.C. For many years, we reflected the diversity of the community, with people from many nations of the world. We were multi-ethnic, but we didn't fully understand what it means to be multi-cultural. God challenged us to think more deeply and to become more intentional—to grow beyond having different people in the room, to fully embrace having different people at the table, and to employ the best of our unique characteristics for the glory of God.

In January of 2020, our church merged with a primarily African American congregation. The pastor and I have become a pastoral team and the lay leaders are becoming a family. We are just at the beginning of this story, but we are growing in our experience of giving glory to God by incorporating the different ways that he made us. This shows up in the meals that we eat, the music that we play, the languages that we speak, and the prayers that we utter.

PRACTICAL EXAMPLES FOR THE CHURCH

Recently, we spent an entire month praying for the needs of people from around the world. Each Sunday, five representatives showed a picture or pictures of their home country and explained what those pictures meant to them. Some were very personal and gave us a glimpse into their family or their home village. Some pictures showed the beauty of the country and places that they would love for us to see. Other pictures pointed to the burdens of their heart—things like natural disasters and political strife. Then they each prayed about what they shared.

Another way that we highlight and enjoy the different cultures in our church is to schedule potluck dinners. Sometimes, we take a particular region of the world and feature food that is unique to a handful of countries. At other times, we just have everyone bring something that represents their cultural tradition, whether it comes from somewhere else in the world or even somewhere else in America. These dinners require that people attend with a willingness to try new things. The result is that others are honored, and respect is shown when their food is enjoyed.

Whatever could cause division can be flipped on its head and celebrated. Even though English is the language that unites us, from time to time, we read scripture and even sing songs in languages that represent our broader community. Once, we put every language group in our church at the front of the sanctuary to read a passage of Scripture, one verse at a time. We call services like this, Voices of Hope.

Any of the above ideas can be experienced by any amount of diversity in the church. All of them represent things that we want the world to see. All of them can become invitation points for people outside the church and outside the faith to come and see a glimpse of heaven and to hear how Jesus is the reason for our hope.

Our newest adventure in cross-cultural evangelism is to offer conversational English gatherings. These can be formal classes or casual meetings where we just get together with people who want to practice their English and become more fluent. These multi-session meetings will allow us to build relationships and explore spiritual needs. Hosting them on Sunday mornings before church will give us a natural opportunity to invite people to stick around for the service.

From an administrative angle, one more idea for the church to consider is to rent space to other ministries when the building is not in use. Too many of our churches sit empty at different times of the week and can be shared, especially with people groups that worship in a language other than English. In our context, we share the building with six other churches, but we do not merely have a landlord and tenant relationship. Instead, we think of each other as ministry partners and work together in a variety of ways, often making the collective result better than just the sum of its parts. In recent years, we have held quarterly discipleship conferences called The Kingdom Project as well as monthly multi-church youth rallies. We especially like to work together on community outreach events where the people that we touch cannot simply be followed up by one church alone.

PRACTICAL EXAMPLES FOR INDIVIDUALS

If you are not in a position of church leadership, you may be wondering what you can do to reach out to people cross-culturally. To begin with, keep in mind that people of another culture can come from anywhere—across the ocean or across the street. Then, with eyes that see your own world as a mission field, you can invite your friends and neighbors to your church, so that they can see what it means and what it looks like to be one in Christ.

To fertilize the soil, though, be sure to build bridges of trust first. If your acquaintance is from another country, ask them how you can pray for their family and the people back home. As you do so, learn about the need. Learn about the joys. Learn about things that give people concern and things that gives them pride. Then pray and remember to keep praying. Follow up your conversations with ongoing interest. In this way, show that you care and then look for opportunities to share the Good News of the Gospel.

To go outside of the box a little, include in your outreach people of different faiths. They certainly don't know it yet, but they need Jesus too. Start with respect. You don't have to agree with people to respect them, and one way to respect them is to ask questions about their faith. If you don't already have a good understanding of what they believe, you can ask with all sincerity as a learner. Quite often, the result is that they, in turn, will ask you about your faith, but don't force this. It will come when the Holy Spirit begins to move in their hearts. In the process of learning about their faith, you might even ask if you could visit their place of worship. After one such visit, one of the men that I met asked me for a Bible. What we think we are beginning, God has already begun. He always goes ahead of us and then moves us to join him on the journey, leading us to people who are hungry to learn more.

All of the above suggestions line up with the heart of Jesus, who looked upon the crowds of people and said, "The harvest is plentiful, but the workers are few. Ask the Lord of the harvest, therefore, to send out workers into his harvest field" (Matthew 9:37–38).

SERVANT EVANGELISM
L. Paulette Jordan

By way of introduction, I am a retired Air Force Logistics Officer who served 24 years on active duty, a college professor for the last 32 years, a Christian educator, praise team leader, choir director, mother, wife, grandmother, sister, and friend. I witnessed for Christ to strangers and friends for the first time as an 11-year-old in Memphis, Tennessee, and those young people were saved!

Evangelism is the act of reaching others for Christ. From the very beginning of the written Word of God in the Book of Genesis, Adam evangelized Eve when he welcomed her into the family of God and respected her as the "Mother of all Creation." By example and practice, Adam introduced Eve to the God who created her and demonstrated the ways in which she could get to know God more intimately and personally. In this capacity as the head of his family, Adam evangelized each of them and facilitated their relationship and service to God.

Today, evangelism for the Kingdom of God takes place in all types and forms. According to Wycliffe Bible Translators, the written Word of God (the entire Bible) has been translated into over 700 languages, the New Testament has been translated into another 1,550 languages, and Bible stories have been translated into another 1,160 languages assisting evangelism efforts worldwide. Modern technology and social media have expanded the reach of the Gospel and evangelism efforts to the far reaches of this planet where the Word of God has been crafted in a strategic way to speak to the hearts of those from diverse and multiple locations. Evangelism of some sort is taking place practically every minute of the day around the world. The two most recent world events (the US withdrawal from Afghanistan and the Russian invasion of Ukraine) highlighted the tenacity and stamina of missionaries who chose to remain in dangerous, war-torn, and hostile environments in order to continue their evangelism and kingdom builders.

Servant evangelism is this level and kind of evangelism. It is rooted and grounded in sacrifice, selflessness, commitment, focus, and determination all in an effort to reach others with the glorious Gospel of Christ. In today's society, to serve someone is considered as being subservient to them or less than. Many of us look upon those who are in the service industry as being beneath us, working for wages that are far less than ours, and doing tasks that are laborious and menial. The scriptures teach another perspective: Jesus said if you want to be great in God's kingdom, you must be a servant of all (Matthew 20:26). He made declarations such as the last shall be first and vice versa. Jesus said that the master should respect the servant and that He came to serve. Servant evangelism then is the culmination of a servant's heart with a lion's strength. It is designed to press through conditions, rejections, objections, and rationale to deliver the sweet love of Christ through a vessel that is yielded to God, responsive to people, and focused on the love and life of Christ. Evangelism that serves the purpose of people, appeals to their heart and need for God, and is based on the love of God personified, this is servant evangelism. Are you a servant evangelist?

Servant evangelism is for any believer who has a burden for souls. Unfortunately, many Christians are operating with the philosophy of "me, myself and mine, all is fine." They are not moved by the number of dying souls that leave this world unprepared to meet God. Servant evangelism flows out of the heart of God's servants who feel the heaviness and burden of lost souls and who have made a life commitment to do something about it.

With all of the million evangelism efforts that go forth each day to lead people to Christ, why is servant evangelism needed, and more importantly, who are the ones who need it the most? Servant evangelism was demonstrated most vividly through the life and ministry of Christ. He sought those who needed a physician and healing for those who were whole and healthy did not need a physician. He crossed religious boundaries and evangelized a Samaritan woman at the well, and she evangelized her whole city (John 4). This was servant evangelism. Jesus healed a blind man, and when His parents were afraid to identify the source of his healing, the man openly declared, "I once was blind, but now I see." His testimony led others to Christ, and Christ was a servant evangelist to heal this unbeliever and send him back to his community. Jesus evangelized a prostitute when it was unholy and unhealthy to have contact with her. She became a pillar of faith and support for His earthly ministry from the point of salvation to being first to witness Him after His resurrection. When a bleeding woman touched the hem of His garment, Jesus's virtue healed her body of a 12-year infirmity, and He evangelized her for the Kingdom. The impact of her healing is not known, but the impact of her healing was undoubtedly known by her physicians, family, community, and village where she was a living testimony of Jesus's healing power for the rest of her days. Jesus went against the traditions of his day to be a servant for a woman in need, and that woman evangelized all who came in contact with her healed body.

So what can you do to become a servant evangelist? We are all too familiar with the local church's feeble efforts at evangelism. Some of them leave tracks in local businesses. Some send out evangelism teams to go door-to-door to "invite people to their church" (not to invite them to Christ). And some send youth and other members to events with signs and fliers to give out to anyone who would take them. These efforts are honorable, but we all know that they are very seldom effective. These types of evangelism best practices have not kept pace with the demand. For our changing society and environment, servant evangelism calls on us to use more intentional and personal strategies to reach the lost. These strategies must go beyond the four walls of the church and into the workplaces, schools, businesses, community organizations, and anywhere the lost sheep have gathered. We must meet them where they are and present the Gospel is a way that appeals to them as to who they are.

While on a leisure trip to Columbus, Georgia, I was invited to listen to a jazz band in a local restaurant; however, when I got there, I became uncomfortable because it was obviously a bar and a club. As a Christian whom the Lord had delivered from such night life, I felt it was inappropriate for me to be there, and I let those around me know it. As I sat there in my self-righteousness, the ladies who had accompanied members of the band sat at my table. As the evening went on, two of us went together to the lady's room. While in there, the young lady began to share about how unhappy she was in her current relationship and that she longed to be loved. I began to share the love of Christ with her and I then led her through the Sinner's Prayer and Romans 10:9–10. She was saved right there in the restroom of a *club*! I did not realize it, but God had transformed me from the traditional forms of evangelism to a servant evangelist that night. I, like Jesus, ignored traditions and focused instead on the lost soul whose hand I was holding.

Servant evangelism requires us to come out of our comfort zones, comfortable places and positions, learned "Christianese," and religious entanglements of all sorts to meet the lost sheep, lost fish, lost people wherever they are. We must sacrifice our own comfort and, yes, beliefs to reach others with the power of the Gospel message. We know of the power of the Gospel; we must discover the ways to deliver it to others without offense or judgement, but through the love of Christ and following His example. So I join with Carolyn Davis and Matthew Davis and the Turning Hearts Ministries to take the Gospel on the go! Servant evangelism is the tool that will give you the creativity, intentionality, determination, and just plain grit to meet the lost sheep around you right where they are…even if that's at a nightclub! Jesus is not afraid of any environment; He went to Hell and took the keys from our enemy. He will be with you as you serve others.

A PERSON WHO THINKS HE'S TOO BAD TO BE SAVED
Marchelle D. Lee

Anyone who knows anything about Third Ward off McGowen Street in Houston, Texas, understands that this one of the most challenging areas for evangelism. On summer while performing outreach activities in the committee with a combination of church volunteers, we decided to go through the neighborhood praying. Well, being delivered from this type of environment, I was not afraid to address most of the gang members and drug dealers in the neighborhood. Many of the residents were receptive to our visits and prayers. However, the ring gang leader and illegal drug supplier (we will call him T. L.), was not happy to see us at all. He had started rounding up his troops before we got to his house, calling them away from the possibility of being talked to in his absence. When we approached his yard, we could feel the anger and resentment for our presence. Not many of the outreach workers wanted to follow me into the yard because they were afraid. However, God gave two other workers (ladies) to accompany me and encouraged us to keep moving in their direction.

At first approach, one could see this young man was the victim of a Spiritual Heart Attack. Blood flow was completely cut off, and he looked cold (cyanotic) and unable to feel anything for condemnation, guilt, and unworthiness. He looked like he did not want to be bothered, no smile, grin, or gesture of welcome and he had a gun in his belt on his right side. I was a little nervous as I got closer and wanted to talk to the others first. But the Holy Spirit said, "This young fellow must be resuscitated first and his body (the group) will follow." God reassured me that the coldness and harsh outward behavior was masking the hurt, broken, and multi-clotted heart, no blood flow appeared to be present.

I ask him to give me a moment with him by himself. He agreed, and the Holy Ghost took over from there. I began to speak into his life as the Holy Spirit gave me revelation. This young man was raised by his grandmother and attended church regularly when she was alive. His mother and father were absent from his life due to riotous living. His grandmother died when he felt he needed her the most, and this led to a downward spiral of life. The streets, gangs, hustling, and crime began to grip him quickly. Survival by any means necessary was his motto and the swinging doors of prison was a way of life for him.

While I was talking and others were silently praying, he started to soften. I know the information being revealed was from God because I never saw T. L. prior to that day. As God spoke, he began to cry and said, "You don't understand the things I have done and the people I have hurt. If they knew what I did just last night, I would be on lockdown right now." I explained there was no sin that was unforgivable in the eyes of the Lord, except dying without repenting and accepting his Son as our Lord and Savior. Scriptures shared with him included, but were not limited to, "All have sinned and come short of the glory of God" (Romans 3:23). "If we say we have no sin, we deceive ourselves, and the truth is not in us. If we confess our sins, he is faithful and just to forgive us our sins and to cleanse us from all unrighteousness" (1 John 8–9).

I explained we all have sinned and God sees and knows, but he is a forgiving Father and can heal all who come to him. One of the ladies on the team stated the Word: "In this, the love of God was made manifest among us that God sent his only Son into the world so that we might live through him. In this is love, not that we have loved God but that he loved us and sent his Son to be the propitiation for our sins" (1 John 4:9–10). Another scripture that was shared with T. L was "You know that he appeared to take away sins, and in him, there is not sin. No one who abides in him keeps on sinning; no one who keeps on sinning has either seen him or know him" (1 John 3:5–6). The young man was crying and saying he hated his life and did not want to live like this. We were able to lead the young man in a prayer of repentance and he asked Jesus to come into his life. We were able to lead several others in the group to Jesus Christ that day. We then asked the men, who had been riding behind us, to come and talk to them and invite them to church, get numbers, etc. It was approximately six churches who were represented that day, and I don't know which church they ended up at, but the seed was planted, and hearts were won.

Fault finding and blame would have destroyed this young man altogether or someone could have seriously gotten hurt. Evangelism sometime is risky; one or more person can lose out. Stoney hearts have huge "Blood Clots" and are difficult; we must take care to avoid trying to use a sledgehammer of judgment or we will become a stumbling block. Most require a long-term relationship with slow doses of anticoagulants (the Word with love) to dissolve them. They must feel that you genuinely are truthful and trustworthy. Remind individuals that they need the salvation that the Word of God says, "Today if ye will hear his voice, harden not your hearts, as in the provocation" (Hebrews 3:15).

NOURISHMENT FOR THE SOUL

CHAPTER 5
Prescribe

The soul winner informs the patient that the best prescription for his condition can only be administered by the Great Physician.

The soul winner is the Pharmacist who fills the prescription according to the doctor's orders. When the patient's condition changes and warrants refills, the Pharmacist advises the patient to contact the Great Physician. Sin is a disease that requires prescriptions that can only be written and prescribed by the Great Physician.

When the soul winner reaches this point in the salvation plan of treatment, he is on the threshold of witnessing a miracle—*salvation* through Jesus Christ!

The Patient's Ailment (Sin)

All men are suffering from a common sickness—S-I-N. Jesus Christ is the Great Physician who can and will heal all mankind from this terminal illness. The soul winner's recommendation in these cases is Jesus and Jesus only.

The Patient's Prescription (Conversion)

The soul winner's prescription is the written Word of God. Discuss the patient's condition with him or her and prescribe the appropriate medication (God's Word). Describe the side effects that the medication will have on his life in the short and long term. The instructions should include: (1) the dosage (read one to three or more dosages of scripture daily), (2) the expiration date (no expiration date; use daily for the rest of your life), and (3) call in for refills (pray to guard against unexpected relapses into sin).

The Patient's Call to Special Action (Repentance)

Ask the patient if he or she has any questions about the written prescription (the Word of God). Ask the patient to believe and accept Jesus as personal Savior.

Lead him or her in this simple prayer of repentance.

Father, I confess that I have sinned and come short of the glory of God. I ask You to forgive me of my sins and to cleanse me from all unrighteousness. I come before You today by faith taking this opportunity to make you my Lord and Savior. I bind Satan and all his demons that would come against me. Lord, I ask you to reign victorious in my life so that I can go forth now in sharing the good news of Your Gospel. Thank You, Father, for opening my eyes and turning me from walking in darkness. I am no longer held captive under the power of Satan. Greater is He that is in me than he that is in the world! Lord, I praise You for saving me and making me an heir and joint heir to Your kingdom, Amen.

Praise God for saving the patient's soul!

The Patient's Affirmation of His Faith (Salvation)

Salvation is a gift of eternal life that can only be attained through the Great Physician, Jesus. Jesus is the doctor and the written prescription always points to the Word of God. Ask him to read aloud Romans 10:9–10 and 1 Corinthians 15:1–5 and reaffirm his faith. Trust God for the results. Once a patient is saved, he or she is always saved. He cannot be plucked out of the ark of safety, Jesus Christ's hand.

Trust God for the Results (Salvation)

The new patient starts out on the milk of the Word. In order for him to graduate to the meat of the Word, he must adhere to a regimented Bible study program. Recommend a Bible teaching church that he can join, and please stress the importance of attending church regularly.

The Patient's Progression (Follow-Up)

As a winner of souls, much is required. Once the patient's condition improves, he or she may be tempted to forego ongoing treatment required to maintain good Christian health, such as studying the Bible, attending church services, getting involved in a Bible study class, joining a Sunday School class, etc. A soul winner should continue to monitor the patient's progress.

Every patient has different needs and the follow-up care varies with each patient. Trust the Great Physician to terminate the soul winner's care. Ask God, and the Spirit will let you know when the patient is strong enough to maintain his own spiritual growth. A soul winner should follow up with the new convert immediately and on a regular basis. Your responsibility does not end once the patient accepts Jesus Christ. As a good physician's assistant, maintain a personal log of those who trusted Jesus for their salvation. Use it to contact, encourage, and pray for and over those you brought to Christ. Use it to remind you of the kingdom building you perform in the name of the Lord and rejoice!

Your Soul Winner's Follow-Up Log should include the patient's name, mailing address, email address, telephone number, date, time, location, and brief description of the salvation experience. Get creative in utilizing this log. For instance, those with similar ailments and sinful conditions can be more effective witnesses to each other. You can ask one of the converts you brought to the Lord to be a witness to someone else you may have failed to reach. You may even want to have a reunion celebration sometime in the future. The possibilities for how you make use of your soul-winner's log are unlimited! Just let the Lord lead you!

MISSIONAL EVANGELISM: THE HEART OF THE MATTER
Herron Wilson

On a recent trip to the grocery store, I was pleasantly surprised to see a former youth Bible student of mine. Mind you, I hadn't seen or visited with him in many years. All grown up and standing six feet tall, he ran up to me and greeted me with a bear hug.

"Rev. Wilson, do you remember me?" he asked.

I replied, "Of course, I do. I was your Bible class teacher many years ago."

The young man's response to that statement literally brought tears to my eyes. In his humble and soft-spoken way, he then said, "Rev. Wilson, you were more than a Bible class teacher to me, you were a father to me."

I could barely restrain the river of tears flowing from my eyes after hearing those heartfelt words.

Could this be the reward for taking the time to introduce him to Jesus? Could this be the young man's way of saying his life is eternally changed because someone dared to care and nurture him spiritually? Could this be God's way of encouraging me to continue reaching people for Him? I asked myself these questions in the days following our visit. I concluded the answer is *yes* to all three. I'm thoroughly convinced that at the heart of evangelism are The Call, The Care, and The Commitment to reach people for Christ.

Having labored in ministry as a pastor and missionary for nearly 30 years, I clearly understand I'm called to do it God's way. If we want God's results, we must do ministry God's Way!

CLEAR CALL

Of all the things Jesus could have said to his disciples prior to ascending to His Father in heaven, he, instead, gave them *a clear call* to evangelize. "Go ye therefore, and teach all nations, baptizing them in the name of the Father, and the Son, and the Holy Ghost. Teaching them to observe all things whatsoever I have commanded you; and lo, I am with you always, even unto the end of the world. Amen" (Matthew 28:19–20).

I must confess that I made the honest mistake, early on in my ministry, of focusing too much on the number of people attending the community mission center. That's not to say we shouldn't be concerned about church growth. We should! Rather, Jesus called his followers, then and now, to make disciples, to reach people and nurture them, both by godly teaching and example, in their personal relationship with the Lord. I find that the more time I spend with people—pouring and investing in their lives—the stronger and more mature they spiritually become. It's abundantly clear that Jesus calls us to build up people in the faith so that they, in turn, can reach and build up others. In this way, the gospel continues to be preached and hearts and lives continue to be transformed eternally.

COMPASSIONATE CARE

I've learned over the years that a clear call to ministry requires me to compassionately care for people. Every person matters to God. He values every individual. At the very heartbeat of God is the desire that every person comes to know Him through faith in Jesus Christ. It blows my mind to know that God wants a personal relationship with each of us as 2 Peter 3:9 says, "The Lord is longsuffering towards us, not willing that any should perish, but that all should come to repentance." Ministry has everything to do with relationship building. We're called to care enough about people's destiny and eternity that we make the time, take the time to introduce them to a growing relationship with the Lord. I've found that to effectively evangelize people for Christ, I have to care enough about them to spend time with them, visit, and offer physical and material help. When necessary, I must offer spiritually encouraging words, pray for and with them, and take the time to inquire about their personal salvation. It takes time, for sure, but it is worth the effort. I've witnessed many people come to the Lord in my ministry all because someone cared enough about them to share the love of God and the message of hope with them.

CONFIDENT COMMITMENT

Evangelism is, without a doubt, an exciting calling. What a privilege it is to join with Jesus in bringing souls to God. In effect, that's what I am, that's what we are, soul winners! The work can be daunting at times, but our Lord calls us to hang in there, to possess a confident commitment to not grow weary in well doing, knowing that at the proper time we will reap a harvest if we do not give up (Galatians 6:9).

During the course of my ministry, I have experienced kidney failure, received a kidney transplant, overcame a stroke, and triumphed over many adversities, thanks to the goodness and grace of God. These temporary illnesses and setbacks cannot be compared to the joy I feel when I see the many lives that have been transformed by the grace and Gospel of Jesus Christ. When I see husbands and wives reconciled in their marriages, youth, whose transformed lives, are making an eternal difference in their schools; men and women living Christ-centered lives, I have to conclude being confidently committed to Christ and His call to evangelize is worth the journey and obedience. My prayer is that more people will answer the clear call, compassionately care for the souls of others, and remain confidently committed to do God's will. For sure, if we do it God's way, we will get God's results!

RURAL EVANGELISM
Richard Booker

I endeavor to put forth a framework for evangelizing in a rural community. This framework will deal with practices that have been used by many rural churches over the years and are still being practiced in rural communities today.

Certain governmental entities will define a rural community in various ways based on population sizes; however, this narrative will not subscribe to a scientific basic as to what a rural community is as it relates to population. If a church is not a part of a metropolitan community, it is generally considered to be a rural church. The people of such communities would be the group that the rural church would set out to evangelize.

This type of evangelism lends itself to be used by churches that may not be trained and equipped to do some other type of evangelism or that partners with some other parachurch ministry. So this method assists in the spreading of the gospel with the intent of winning souls for Christ.

The type of rural evangelism that has been used by the church that I am a part of and many other churches similarly situated is as follows: as an evangelism campaign is anticipated, the church is called to prayer. The normal length of the prayer service is at least one week; however, this may vary and carry on longer. Typically, the church will meet nightly at the church for this purpose. The theme of the prayers may include prayer for being able to contact as many of the unsaved and unchurched as possible, prayer for the one doing the preaching. The overall theme is generally "Lord, Send a Revival."

As the prayer meeting is taking place, congregants are busy reaching out to people that they are aware of that are unsaved or unchurched. Being in a rural setting, very often, people are more familiar with who their neighbors are and even if they profess a hope in Christ. The people are invited to attend the revival and are in a sense the unsaved are being brought to the gospel. Again, these parishioners may not feel comfortable handling the word of God in a witnessing situation, but have the relationships and people skills to interest someone in attending a revival.

Transportation is a part of the equation when it comes to this type of evangelism. Many times, there is a youth component involved in such a meeting, and transportation is provided to pick up the youth and carry them to the meeting. I have experienced what I call an extra layer of fellowship in the transportation piece. Often, people will get started singing while they are traveling to and from the revival meeting. This can add joy to those individuals using the transportation that has been provided.

An old practice used by churches was known as canvasing the house. People were asked if they were saved or not and would be put on notice that the church was praying for them that they would receive the Lord Jesus Christ as their Savior. Some rural churches still practice canvasing.

The method of evangelism described above has proven to be effective time and time again. One of the most successful revivals I have experienced, as far as souls coming to Christ, was conducted in this manner. People were reached and decisions were made.

Just to add a flavor of celebration to this process, allow me to talk about the baptism that would take place after one of these successful campaigns. Typically, churches will come together for the purpose of baptizing candidates. Various outdoor venues were used as a place to baptize, such as lakes, rivers, and sometime watering holes. The pageantry of such baptisms added to the symbolism that Paul called for in Romans chapter 3.

STORYTELLING EVANGELISM
Sally Hinzie

Bible Storying is a way to present the gospel and disciple oral learners. It has been estimated that over half of the world's population are oral learners; this includes the United States. Even if a person is functionally or semi-literate, they still prefer oral methods. Oral learners take in life-changing information through the non-written word! They learn through narratives, stories, and the arts including music, drama, and poetry. Handing an oral learner, a Bible will not bring about life change.

Missionaries working in countries where there is no printed gospel available in the heart language of the people use a method called storying to present the gospel message. Story sets have been created that address bridges and barriers to the gospel. A story set for women created to introduce them to the love and provision of God would include Eve, Sarah, Hagar (especially in Muslim cultures), Rachel and Leah, Ruth, Esther, the woman with the issue of blood, the Samaritan woman at the well.

A story set that presents the gospel starts in Genesis with the creation of the world and the fall of man, the story continues with promises to Abraham and into Exodus to include Passover and the Ten Commandments. Prophecies about the coming Messiah are included. The Annunciation and birth of Jesus are told, showing the fulfillment of prophecies about Jesus's birth. Stories of Jesus's miracles showing that He had the authority to forgive sin and has power over nature, power over demons, and power over death. Events leading up to the crucifixion and the crucifixion story include: the Resurrection and all the witnesses that give proof to the Resurrection. The Ascension places Jesus at the right hand of God. The stories can be told back-to-back at one time or in a succession of meetings.

Discussion of the stories can help the listener process the biblical truths. I like to use a six-question format including:

1. What do you like about this story?
2. What don't you like about this story?
3. What don't you understand about this story?
4. What did you learn about God (or Jesus—depending on the story) in this story?
5. What do you want to do differently after hearing this story?
6. What part of this story do you want to continue to think about this week?

You can tell a narrative version of these stories in one setting. I heard it called Creation to Christ. This story can be told in fifteen minutes or forty minutes or any time frame in between the two. The time frame would determine how many details you can include. It is the gospel. I can tell you, the first time I heard this presented by one of my instructors, I was amazed. I remember thinking, *I will never be able to do that.*

We befriend international students at the University of Houston. Our commitment is to meet with them once a month. Often, we meet with them in our home and have dinner. The first night we had Q over, he saw the Bibles on our coffee table and wanted to know the abbreviated version of what the Bible is about. I could only pray, "Please help me, Holy Spirit," and I jumped right into a Creation to Christ presentation. I had never done this before, and I certainly had no advance notice to practice. I remembered all the key points and it went well. Over dinner, he asked about the differences between the different Christian groups. I told him it would be easier if I told him what we had in common and launched into Creation to Christ again. I was able to present the gospel to Q twice that night because he asked!

Fast forward a couple of years and we have a new Chinese student, C. We had driven out to the country to have dinner with friends so C could see the countryside. A rainstorm had moved in while we were eating, so I was driving her back to her dorm in the rain. As we drove by a couple of different churches on I-10, C asked what was the difference between all the Christian churches. That was my cue. Leonard, my husband, knew what was going to come next and immediately started praying. I knew I had about fifteen minutes before we arrived at her dorm. Thank God for the rain because traffic was moving slowly and I could take my time. Again, I said it would be easier for me to share what we had in common and launched into Creation to Christ. When I finished, there was silence. I was driving and could not make eye contact. I waited a few minutes and said, "Well?"

C responded, "I am silent because I am shocked."

I asked if it was a good shock or a bad shock.

C said, "I am shocked because I have never heard anything like this before in my life. Chinese people do not know these things."

In the few minutes left, we discussed how one could know there really was a God. She was studying microbiology and was able to prove it to herself when she talked about the miracle of a cell in the human body.

Another time we were having a children's club in a predominantly Muslim apartment complex. I chose four Quran-friendly Bible stories to share with the children. One for each night: Creation, Annunciation to Mary, Birth of Jesus, and Jesus healing the paralyzed man. On Wednesday night, S, an eight-year-old Pakistani Muslim girl, asked for more stories. She loved hearing the stories. I knew the Quran taught Jesus did miracles, so I thought it would be safe to tell her the stories of Jesus's miracles that we tell our children. I told her about blind Bartimaeus, feeding the five thousand, walking on water, and calming the storm among others the Spirit called to mind. After about fifteen minutes of stories, S looked up at me and asked, "Is Jesus God?"

God's Word does not return empty. If an eight-year-old Pakistan Muslim girl can figure this out, anyone can. God's Word promises, "As the rain and the snow come down from heaven, and do not return to it without watering the earth and making it bud and flourish, so that it yields seed for the sower and bread for the eater, so is my word that goes out from my mouth: It will not return to me empty, but will accomplish what I desire and achieve the purpose for which I sent it" (Isaiah 55:10–11).

JUST TELL THE STORY! A PERSON
WHO HAS A TERMINAL DISEASE
Marchelle D. Lee

Often, this is probably the easiest person of all to win to the Lord. When people are dying, they are fearful about the dying process and what is next. The Word of God tells us explicitly that there is a heaven and a hell. "For the wages of sin is death, but the gift of God is eternal life" (Romans 6:23). Dying people wonder if God will punish them for life's failures, mistakes, and sin. It is a great time to witness because most people want to make it right with God and their loved ones.

In my thirty-year tenure as a registered nurse, myself and the staff that I have worked with have led countless dying individuals to Christ, both young and old. This is the most crucial and opportune time to make sure a person is confident with their transition from this world to the next. The youngest dying person I (we) have ever won to Jesus was sixteen years of age and the oldest was ninety. Consider these scriptures when ministering to those who are at the end-of-life process:

> For I am sure that neither death nor life, nor angels nor rulers, nor things present nor things to come, nor powers, nor height nor depth, nor anything else in all creation, will be able to separate us from the love of God in Christ Jesus our Lord. (Romans 8:38–39)

> Jesus said to her, "I am the resurrection and the life. Whoever believes in me, though he die, yet shall he live, and everyone who lives and believes in me shall never die. Do you believe this?" (John 11:25–26)

> That if thou shalt confess with thy mouth the Lord Jesus, and shalt believe in thine heart that God hath raised him from the dead, thou shalt be saved. (Romans 10:9)

> For whosoever shall call upon the name of the Lord shall be saved. (Romans 10:13)

Unsaved dying people have a receptive heart for the most part and are usually surrounded by loved ones at the end of life. If they are in the normal process of dying, they are tired of living and want to leave their present state. They are more than likely to be open to conversation and making sure "they have no unfinished business." This is not always the case, but no matter what it is the Christian's responsibility to make sure you offer Jesus to a passing person, if you are not sure that Jesus is his or her Savior.

No matter what, salvation is free to all who will believe and accept Jesus into their life. It is an individual choice, and no one can receive it, but the one in need of it. We are never too young or too old to ask Christ into our lives. If the steps below are covered, God is willing to be reconciled with his humanity.

- First, one must admit that they are a sinner and need to be saved.
- Second, one must repent and be willing to turn from their sin.
- Third, one must believe that Jesus Christ died for them on the cross.
- Fourth, one must receive, through prayer, Jesus Christ into their heart and life.

Confrontational evangelism is another method for winning souls to the Lord, yet it is the least recommended in today's time. As a class, we will discuss what it is and why in times past it worked and yet today is the least suggested. As well as who would most benefit from this approach in today's time.

THE BILINGUAL WITNESS
ACTS 8:26–40
Matthew A. Davis

It was a hot summer morning in June. I had completed a twelve-hour shift and a shift meeting. By this time, it was 10:00 a.m. and 90° Fahrenheit. I was traveling west on Highway 225, going home. Yes, I was weaving in and out of traffic in my usual way, when I looked to my left and I saw on the other side of the freeway a lady standing outside her car, with a baby standing on the back seat, and the hood was up. Obviously, this lady was in danger, her car had stopped on the side of a road, and the baby was inside a car in 90° plus temperatures. I took the next exit, made a U-turn, and pulled up behind the car. I stopped my car, put it in park, and began to walk toward her car, when I noticed a man leaning over into the hood of the car. I thought, had I known that there was a man present, I would have kept driving west. Well, since I was there, I decided to assist in any way I could. We were unable to get the car started; therefore, it became my responsibility to take them to Baytown, Texas. There was a tunnel that led from Baytown to Laporte, Texas, at that time by way of the tunnel. We went to Baytown and came back.

During the trip, I was advised by the wife that the man did not speak English. Therefore, I engaged in a spiritual conversation with the wife, but made sure she told her husband everything I said. I was also informed by the wife that she was born again, but her husband was not. Man, God threw the door to witnessing wide open! It became my duty to be the catalyst that God would use for this man's salvation experience. Because I was very weak in my Spanish language, I had to speak English to the lady and have her to speak Spanish to her husband. By this time, we were on our way back and headed into the tunnel. I asked his wife to ask him if he knew Jesus Christ as a savior. He said no! I told him that Jesus Christ is the Son of God, and out of obedience to God, he gave his life as a ransom for him and me.

I told him that over 2000 years ago, Jesus Christ lived a sinless life and died on a hill called Calvary. I told him that men nailed His hands and His feet. I continued by telling him that He died on a cross on that hill that day. Men took him off the cross and buried his dead body in an unused tomb. I further told him, early morning on the third day, Jesus rose from the dead with all power in heaven and earth in his hands. I continued to let him know that the same power that raised up this dead Jesus can save him today. I asked him did he believe this story. He said, "Yes, I believe this story." I asked him if he would invite Christ into his life. He said yes. By that time, we were in the middle of the tunnel headed back up out of the tunnel. During this whole conversation, I was speaking through his wife. She was speaking English to me. I was speaking English to her. She speaking Spanish to him. He was speaking Spanish to her, and she was telling me in English just what he said. This man entered the tunnel from the east in my car as an unsaved soul. But when we came out of the tunnel, he was a born-again man in Jesus Christ. Hallelujah to the lamb! This is another soul that Jesus has turned around, renewed his life by using bilingual communication. Thank God for his ability to save all men, regardless of ethnicity, culture, or background.

THE HOMELESS MAN WITNESS
1 CORINTHIANS 15:1–5
Matthew A. Davis

Between the years of 1985 and 1999, I was given the opportunity to preach at a homeless shelter in Houston, Texas. During these years, I saw many guys come and go from that shelter. My mission was to continue to preach Jesus Christ and Him crucified. As a result, I witnessed the change of many men and gave their lives to Jesus the Christ. My preaching always challenged men to get to know Jesus. For many years, I noticed one particular young man who always sat in the far back of the building. He always looked mean and disturbed. He would never smile. He would never interact with the other men or church members. This young man would just stare at me and never respond to the gospel. But I continued to preach the gospel.

After several years of preaching at this homeless shelter, this guy finally walked up to me, with tears in his eyes. And he said to me, "Year after year, I watched you come to this shelter and only preach one thing and that was the Gospel of Jesus Christ." I consistently spoke of the death, burial, and resurrection of Jesus Christ and how one's trust in this story can and will make a man whole. He continued, "Man, I got sick and tired of you telling the same story every single Monday night for the last seven years. I really, really, really hated you. I wanted to kill you. The more you preached Jesus, His crucifixion, and resurrection, the more I thought the worst of you. I have been plotting and trying to find a way to take your life without going to prison. But now I understand. You were only here to help us gain our salvation from Jesus Christ. I just want to tell you, because of your continual preaching of the uncompromising gospel, I have accepted Jesus as my savior tonight. I no longer want to hurt you. I only want to show my appreciation to you. Man, I love you. Thank you for allowing the Lord to use you. He has saved my soul. I have fallen in love with the Gospel of Jesus Christ, and it is all because you continued preaching the same story, repeatedly. Thank you, my brother. Now I am on my way to heaven."

THE POLICE WITNESS
ROMANS 8:28
Matthew A. Davis

One night, I was at home alone, and suddenly, there was a knock at the door. Standing there was a police officer named David. I opened the door and invited him in. Once on the inside, the police officer told me that he was answering a call about a disturbance. I gave him the freedom to look around. He then realized I was at home alone, and there was no disturbance in the house. In the process of his looking around, he noticed my Bible on the kitchen countertop. He asked me was I a believer in Jesus Christ. I answered yes. From that point on, it was on. It was one testimony after another of God's goodness. He turned his radio down, and we began to talk about Jesus the Christ. Yes, iron was sharpening iron. It was such an amazing experience. Before we realized it, an hour had passed by.

Suddenly, there was another knock at the door. It was the second police officer name Raul. You see because David had turned the volume down on his radio, dispatch was unable to reach him. Therefore, they dispatched Raul to check on him. After Raul stated his case and his reason for being there, we begin to talk to him about Jesus the Christ, also. Yes, God blessed us that night. During our discussion about Jesus Christ, we discovered that he was not saved. So David and I began to share Jesus Christ with Raul. During the process, we were able to walk Raul through the plan of salvation. We led Raul to Christ, standing right there in my living room. Oh, what a joy it was. There I was, standing in my living room with two police officers. One officer came into the house saved. The other officer came into the house unsaved. But because of God's amazing grace, that night, I was standing in that room with two police officers, both saved brothers in Jesus the Christ. Glory be to God! He takes the worst of things and make them good!

WELCOME TO GOD'S SOUL-WINNING TEAM!

If you participated in this course to develop and utilize your soul winning skills, congratulations on completing this course and welcome to God's soul-winning team!

If you accepted Jesus as your Lord and Savior during this course, congratulations! Making this life-changing decision is the most important one you will ever make. Welcome to the family of God and remember:

No one can take eternal life away from you. "And I give eternal life to them, and they shall never perish; and no one shall snatch them out of my hand" (John 10:28).

Join a Bible teaching church where you can grow as a Christian. Heed the warning against "not forsaking or neglecting to assemble together, as is the habit of some, but encouraging one another" (Hebrews 10:25).

CLASS ASSIGNMENT

Write a letter presenting the Gospel to a friend, loved one, or family member who has not accepted Jesus as Lord and Savior. Perhaps you will say something in this letter that will compel someone to ask you, "What do I need to do to be saved?" This act of love could be your first soul winning opportunity. Remember, if you do not use it (what you have learned in this course), you will lose it.

Bearing in mind that the focus is on salvation only, utilize what you have learned about soul winning and choose one of these scenarios to demonstrate how a soul winner can overcome challenges in leading a person to Christ. Practice using the scenarios below.

1. A person who's angry with God
2. A good person who thinks he is saved, but is not
3. A suicidal person
4. A person who thinks he is too bad to be saved
5. A person who has a terminal disease
6. A person who thinks God is too good to send someone to hell
7. A person who does not believe in the religious system
8. A person who has been disappointed by those who are in church
9. A person who knows too many Christians who are hypocrites
10. A person who believes there is no God

NOURISHMENT FOR THE SOUL

"All men suffer from a common sickness—sin. Jesus Christ is the Great Physician who can and will heal us of this sickness."
—Matthew A. Davis, 1998

TERMINOLOGY

Adamic Nature: The natural, sensual, and sinful life of mankind; related to Adam and his disobedience to God (1 Corinthians 2:14).

Baptism: The process of submerging a person underwater as a visible testimony of a new birth experience. It is the way of showing that you have been washed free of sin by the death and rising from the dead of Jesus Christ.

Christian: A follower of Christ; one who trusts Jesus as his Lord and Savior; a disciple.

Church:
- The Bride of Christ, those who trust the death, burial, and resurrection of Jesus Christ.
- The building designated for worshipping God.
- The atmosphere of experiencing God.

Discipleship: The process of training a follower of Jesus Christ.

Doctor: Jesus the Christ who heals us of our ailment—sin.

Evangelism: The process of spreading the gospel that men may be turned toward God.

God: The object of our worship; our creator and sustainer; the first person of the triune Godhead.

Godhead: God; the deity.

God's Word: The Holy Bible. It contains God's will and purpose for mankind.

Heart: The inner self that thinks, feels, wills, and decides; the seat of affections.

Holy Spirit: The third person of the trinity who exercises the power of the Father and the Son in creation and in redemption; the Spirit of God through whom men receive power.

Hope: Confident expectation. Essential to our perseverance and getting through the tough times requires trust in Jesus Christ.

Jesus Christ:
- A. The human divine Son of God; Savior of the world.
- B. The second person of the trinity

Love: The high esteem that God has for mankind and we should in turn have for God and other people.

Ministry: Duty or service to God.

Patient: The listener; the one who hears the testimony of the soul winner and receives the Word of God.

Salvation: Redemption and deliverance from the power of sin.

Soul Winner: One who testifies of God's goodness and encourages others to believe the plan of salvation.

Trinity: God in three persons—God the Father, God the Son, and God the Holy Spirit.

Witness:
- The person who has experienced the saving power of Jesus Christ and testifies to it.
- The testimony of one's belief in Jesus Christ.

Turning Hearts Ministries (THM)
Presents
THEM
Turning Hearts Evangelistic Ministries
2 Chronicles 16:9; Acts 1:8
Lesson Plan/Nourishment for the Soul

Scriptures must support all assignments.

- Write a 15 to 30 line essay describing your salvation experience.
- Study the key scriptures. Choose two and memorize.
- Study main scriptures and interpret them in your own words. (Use a Concordance and Bible only.)
- Study and memorize one of these tracts: "The Roman Road" or "The Four Spiritual Laws."
- Review and study your notes; prepare to take the midterm exam.
- Using Psalm 51 as your point of reference; write an eight to ten line prayer of repentance.
- Write a letter presenting the Gospel to a friend, loved one, or family member who has not accepted Jesus as Lord and Savior.
- Review and study your notes.
- Prepare to take the final exam.
- Take open book test facilitated by the classroom instructor.
- 100% class participation is required.

NOURISHMENT FOR THE SOUL

TURNING HEARTS EVANGELISTIC MINISTRIES (THEM)
(AN EVANGELISTIC DISCIPLESHIP PROGRAM FOR THE ENTIRE COMMUNITY)
"TURNING HEARTS TOWARD GOD"

2 CHRONICLES 16:9; ACTS 1:8; MALACHI 4:6; EZEKIEL 22:30

Sharing the Gospel, Good News on the Go is the first of seven publications to be released by Matthew A. Davis. Similar to **Sharing the Gospel**, the next six publications will be based on the Bible study courses taught at THEM. At THEM, we use these Bible study courses to train, equip, educate, and develop participants in soul winning techniques and Christian discipleship.

Sharing the Gospel. This course teaches students how to share their faith in the Gospel of Jesus Christ, as they are assured of their salvation.

Teaching the Gospel. After completing the **Sharing the Gospel** course, the students will exercise their discipleship skills and apply what they have learned by teaching the course to others.

Counseling through the Gospel. This course teaches students how to utilize biblical principles in counseling others through the challenges of life and everyday living.

Living the Gospel. This course focuses on fellowship and stewardship. After completing the first four courses, students are accountable to God, themselves, and others. The students are paired off to strengthen and assess each other's Christian character and integrity.

Preaching the Gospel. This course consists of Hermeneutics, Homiletics, and Bible study methods in order to sharpen the skills of the pastor and the preacher/teacher.

Defending the Gospel. People perish for a lack of knowledge in the Word of God. This course stresses the importance of understanding cults and religious groups (deceptive beliefs and religious practices). It teaches participants how to "try the spirit by the Spirit." The focus is equipping believers to validate true Christianity and compare it against false prophecy and false prophets.

THEM Presents the Sharing the Gospel Workbook in Eight Languages

English ....Matthew and Carolyn Davis
Portuguese... Charles and Marcia Barbosa
Spanish...Florentino Rubio and Ben Garza
Swahili ....Richard and Flora Maabadi
Luhya .... Dolly Ifetha
Czech...Milca Kmochova
French ....Mwamba Kataku Justin
Hindi .... John Sanjay

NOURISHMENT FOR THE SOUL

TURNING HEARTS MINISTRIES
2 CHRONICLES 16:9; ACTS 1:8; MALACHI 4:6

Our History

As a para-ministry (para-church), Turning Hearts Ministries acknowledges that family, church, school, and community are the primary institutions for Christian growth and discipleship. This ministry strives to influence all four institutions through evangelism, Christian counseling, and referral services. As the physical heart is the central, essential, and innermost organ of the human body, so is the spiritual heart the most vital component in one's spiritual life. It is the spiritual heart that controls one's character, feelings, and inclinations. Once a man's heart is turned toward God, he is never the same, only better (Romans 10:9; 2 Corinthians 5:17). Thus, we have derived the name, Turning Hearts Ministries.

Our Vision

- To fulfill the Great Commission by sharing love, hope, and God's Word with all mankind (Matthew 28:19–20)
- To encourage Christian well-being and high self-esteem (Psalms 139:14; Philippians 4:13)
- To improve family life, life skills, affordable housing, and family values (Ephesians 6:4; Ezekiel 22:30)
- To combat deterioration of the family and juvenile delinquency (Proverbs 22:6)

Our Mission

- To edify the body of Christ, uplift the name of Jesus, and glorify God the Father through the empowerment of the local church.
- To proclaim the Good News of Jesus the Christ.

- To educate the world through the preaching, teaching, worshiping, and dramatization of the Gospel.
- To encourage and exhort men to become Christian mentors for young people through Christian guidance, instruction, and leadership (live the word through exemplary roles and lifestyles).
- To teach the Christian body how to witness effectively for Jesus Christ.
- To guide youth in sharing their faith comfortably in environments outside of the church congregations including schools, colleges, organizations, etc.
- To counsel individuals in restoring and maintaining relationships with God through active participation in church ministry.

NOURISHMENT FOR THE SOUL

TURNING HEARTS MINISTRIES, INC. (THM)

Established October 7, 1997
Phone: 713-905-9767
Emails:
Dr. Matthew A. Davis, TurningHearts@yahoo.com
Dr. Marchelle D. Lee, MDLMinistries1@gmail.com
PO Box 503 Missouri City, Texas 77459

Dads of Faith is supported by male Christian mentors such as fathers, uncles, brothers, cousins, and guardians who provide guidance, instruction, and leadership to other males through Christian values.

Dads USA is a support group for fathers. The focus is father-child bonding. It reaches out to fathers throughout the surrounding communities, schools, and judiciary systems.

THM Literacy Center provides tutoring assistance, both academically and spiritually, for children of single and working parents.

Turning Hearts Evangelistic Ministries (THEM) is an evangelistic program for the Christian Community. Its purpose is to train, educate, equip, and develop Christians in soul winning.

Turning Hearts Music and Drama Ministry is a youth outreach ministry that ministers to the homeless and convalescent community through music and drama. It focuses on fine arts.

Turning Hearts Institute is the educational branch of the ministry. Training, instruction, and mentoring are offered for life skills and Science, Technology, Engineering, Arts, and Math (STEAM) Programs. These programs include: robotics, music, performing arts, economics, hydroponics, and aquaponics.

NOURISHMENT FOR THE SOUL

CONTRIBUTING AUTHORS

Brian Bakke grew up in inner-city Chicago. He attended Wake Forest University on a football scholarship. He majored in theater and gained a minor in studio arts. His art work has been exhibited in Chicago, Washington, DC, and New York City and is in private collections in Asia and Latin America and the USA. Brian worked at Uptown Baptist Church as the Outreach Pastor from 1987 to 2001. As such, he directed the church's ministry to the homeless, artists, street gangs, mentally disabled, HIV infected, and successfully led a vote dry campaign to remove illegal liquor stores in the neighborhood. Brian also led New Flight Arts which used the arts to reach children, senior adults, gangs, homeless, men in prison, and professional artists. Currently, Brian works as the Director of the Americas for the Mustard Seed Foundation. This position takes him to the major cities of the Western Hemisphere in search of partnerships with small local congregations that are reaching their neighbors for God. For the past 20 years, Brian and his wife Lisa have lived in Washington, DC.

Richard Booker has been the Pastor of Little Zion Baptist Church in Kendleton, Texas, for the past 47 years. Pastor Booker attended Arkansas AM&N College at Pine Bluff, where he received a Bachelor of Science Degree. Since graduating from Arkansas AM&N, Pastor Booker has studied at Prairie View A&M University and Southwestern Theological Seminary of New Orleans. Pastor Booker received a Master of Arts in Theological Studies and a Doctorate Degree in Expository Communication from Faith Evangelical Seminary in

Tacoma, Washington. Along with being Pastor of Little Zion Baptist Church, he is an adjunct professor at Oikodome Bible Institute. Pastor Richard Booker is married to Sharon, and they have five children and three grandchildren.

Sharon Booker is a Christian woman of God who intensely loves the Lord with all of her being. She is the beloved wife of Reverend Dr. Richard Booker, Pastor of Little Zion Missionary Baptist Church in Kendleton, Texas. They are the proud parents/ grandparents of five children and three grandchildren. Sharon is a member at Little Zion where she currently serves in the following capacities: Servant Leader for the Women's Ministry, Member of the Praise Ministry, and Facilitator for Sunday Church School. Sharon is a sought-after conference speaker who delivers God's Word with conviction, passion, and honesty. She has been blessed to share with the following conferences to name a few: CEED Workshop and Retreat, Silver-Lake Women's Conference, and Oikodome Bible Conference. Sharon is a graduate of Faith Seminary located in Tacoma, Washington, where she received a Master of Arts in Christian Ministry. She retired from the telecommunications field as a Senior Software Specialist. Sharon is a certified facilitator for both the PREP marriage curriculum, Within Our Reach, and a Hospice Volunteer. Her motto is "Jesus first, Jesus second, and Jesus third in my life."

Carolyn Orr Davis is a graduate of Jackson State University where she received her Bachelor of Music in Education Degree (BME) in 1982. For twenty-nine years, Mrs. Davis taught at Dodson Elementary and Montessori School in which she organized a Recorder and Xylophone Ensemble who performed in and around the Houston area and at the Music Teachers' Convention in San Antonio, Texas (TMEA). Students learned self-discipline, perseverance, and high self-esteem. These are life-long traits students needed to be productive citizens in life. Mrs. Davis's students were great musicians, but she wanted more for her students. She wanted them to know about God. She believed that if she got the students hooked on music, she could tell them about Jesus Christ, and they could have a better life. So she started having Summer Music Enrichment Camps for the sole purpose of leading youths to Christ. From 2014-2020, Mrs. Davis taught at Field Elementary School. In May of 2020, Mrs. Davis retired from the school system, but continues to teach music and tell children about Christ—thus her motto then and now is "Reaching Youth for Christ through Music."

Allen R. Grimes, Jr. serves as the Executive Pastor of First Alliance Church in Silver Spring, Maryland. First Alliance is a multi-racial and multi-national congregation with people from countries worldwide. Pastor Grimes served as Senior Pastor of Harvest Time Community Church until its merger with First Alliance in January 2020. He is also the Founder and Executive Director of Amazing Grace Culinary and Etiquette Program (AGCEP), a nonprofit program established to serve youth within the Washington Metropolitan area, teaching social and leadership skills. He is a proud member of Phi Beta Sigma Fraternity, Inc. Pastor Grimes attended Liberty University where he received a degree in Business Administration. He is continuing his studies in Christian Leadership and Management with an emphasis on Pastoral Care. Reverend Grimes and his wife Debra have been married and served in ministry for 29 years. They have two wonderful children.

Sally Hinzie is a Church/Ministry Consultant at Union Baptist Association in Houston, Texas. She is a veteran of over 30 overseas mission trips, studying cultures and using storying methods. Sally's primary areas of ministry focus include: Church Planting, Bible Storying Training, Organic Church, and Ministry Implementation. She is married to Leonard Hinzie. They have two adult children and one granddaughter.

Jeffery D. Jackson has served as an Outreach and Children's Minister at Brown Missionary Baptist Church (BMBC) in Southaven, Mississippi, since May 2001. Mr. Jackson earned his Bachelor's Degree from The University of Alabama in Computer Information Systems and Business Administration. As a part of BMBC outreach ministry, Mr. Jackson has been afforded the opportunity to travel the world, proclaiming the gospel of Jesus Christ to men, women, boys, and girls, instilling hope in hopeless situations. Mr. Jackson is the creator of The T-shirt Gospel Kit, a tool used to share the gospel using minature/ colorful t-shirts that takes an unbeliever from the creation of man to the death, burial, and resurrection of Jesus Christ. Mr. Jackson is married to a wonderful wife, Linda Williams Jackson, who is an author. He is also the proud father of two daughters, Oliva and Chloe, and one son, Benjamin.

L. Paulette Jordan has served as a Bible Study leader, choir member, Sunday School teacher, and lay leader in the church for over 50 years. She has spent over fifty years singing and directing choirs, leading praise and worship, and hosting top names in Gospel Music including Willie Sommerville, the late Walter Hawkins, John P. Kee, the late Donnie McClurkin, and Kirk Franklin. Professionally, she is a Doctoral Program Director at a private Christian university in Dallas. She has been in higher education since 1987.

Dr. Jordan is a retired Air Force Logistics Officer who served on active duty for 24 years and achieved the rank of Major. She holds a Bachelor of Science Degree in Business Education from the University of Memphis and four master's degrees: an MBA from Liberty University, a Master of Science in Human Organizational Science from Villanova University; a Master of Arts in Religious Studies from Liberty Theological Seminary, and a Master of Science in Entrepreneurial Management from Stratford University. In September 2013, she received the Doctor of Education Degree with distinction (4.0 GPA) from Liberty University and is currently working on a Doctor of Ministry where she is researching the church's response to adults with disabilities. In addition to her professional and academic achievements, Dr. Jordan worked alongside her husband as a ministry team for eight gospel services. Paulette is married to Army Chaplain (Lieutenant Colonel, Retired) Steven L. Jordan Sr. They have two daughters, one son, and two grandchildren.

Pam Lilly has served in ministry since 2008 with Faith Comes by Hearing, StoryRunners, a ministry of Cru, and currently Mission Increase as an Area Director in Houston, Texas. Pam is a graduate and coach for the Master's Program for Women and serves on the Fellowship of Barnabas Partners board. She is the author of *Mary Morning Martha Day,* translated in English, Spanish, and Amharic. She is a contributing writer for *YOU*, a publication of Lifeway Christian Recourses. Pam lives in Houston, Texas, with her husband, Chester. They have three adult children and five grandchildren, who they enjoy pouring into with the love of God.

Ayanna Alexis Lynn received a basketball scholarship from Itawamba Community College where she majored in Engineering. After she graduated from Itawamba Community College, she went on to further her education at Jackson State University on a full basketball scholarship and received Bachelor's and Master's Degrees in Engineering. Ayanna worked as a Process Engineer at Nissan North America in Canton, Mississippi. She also worked at Ford Motor Company in Chicago as a Product Development Engineer and a Senior Industrial Engineer. Ayanna's second master's degree is the Master of Business Administration. She is the founder of Ayanna Real Estate Development and Ayanna's Trucking Company.

Ayanna provides leadership at all levels. She believes in giving back to her community and motivating other individuals to achieve their dreams and future aspirations. As for the future, Ayanna will continue to serve in her community by sponsoring a youth basketball camp in the summer. This event is free to the community in her hometown, Indianola, Mississippi. In October of 2018, Ayanna published her first book entitled *Success Takes Time*. Her motivation for writing *Success Takes Time* was to let her readers know in order to be successful you will go through trials and tribulations. She also wants her readers to never give up on themselves no matter where they are in life. Ayanna is now working on her second book *Loving the Wrong Man* which she plans to publish in 2022.

Dr. Bryan McCabe serves as a pastor at North Way Christian Community (NWCC) in the city of Pittsburgh, Pennsylvania. In this role, he leads the East Liberty Ministry Hub and he directs North Way's strategic urban partnerships with the House of Manna Faith Community in the Homewood neighborhood of Pittsburgh and the Learning and Mentoring Partnership (LAMP) youth mentoring initiative. He is the founder and director of the Transformational Urban Leadership Institute at NWCC. Bryan is also the Academic Dean and Chief Academic Officer at Bakke Graduate University where he equips urban leaders on six continents.

Dr. Michael J. Mercurio has served as the lead pastor of First Alliance Church in Silver Spring, Maryland, since June of 2005. The church is multi-racial and multi-national with people from more than 20 countries of the world. Pastor Mercurio earned his Doctor of Ministry Degree at Asbury Theological Seminary in Wilmore, Kentucky, in 2007. His dissertation is titled, "The Fruit of the Spirit and the Incarnational Nature of the Missional Church." Pastor Mike (as he prefers to be called) is married to Carrol and they have three children with seven grandchildren. Together, they have served five congregations over more than 40 years, in New York, Kentucky, Illinois, New Jersey, and Maryland.

Arletha Orr is an American author from a small town in Mississippi. Orr initially started working a corporate job until exasperated by it, and she eventually ventured into full-time entrepreneurship until she realized that destiny had other plans for her. It was only when her world collapsed around her, after a fatal evening that Arletha discovered her true calling in life. She knew that God had a greater purpose for her and with Him by her side, Orr began her journey to shine a light for the people whose lives had been consumed by the darkness around them. With her passion and vigor, she hopes to selflessly serve others and save souls for God's Kingdom. Orr is an author and publisher of the book *Live*. Orr is working to finish the children book on grief called *Best Friends Forever*. She's also a Certified Life Coach who has answered the call of God on her life to inspire and encourage those around her. Arletha Orr is also the Founder and Chief Operations Officer of Kingdom Trailblazers Publishing.

Richard Jewel Rose has served as Pastor of Holy Trinity Missionary Baptist Church of Houston, Texas, for more than 50 years. He is also the president of Oikodome Bible Institute. Dr. Rose has an extended educational background in both religious and secular education. He has attended and received degrees from the following colleges, universities, and seminaries: East Carolina College, Cascades of Glory Bible Tabernacle, Union Theological Seminary, Houston Community College (AA), March of Faith Bible Institute (BTh), Texas Southern University (BA), Houston Graduate School of Theology (MATS), and Faith Evangelical Seminary (MDiv, DMin). He is the proud husband of Sundrell and the father of two adult children.

Lawrence Scott is the planting and Lead Pastor of Harvest Point Fellowship Church. His ministry experience spans many years, serving in various positions within the local church. Lawrence is a man who values family. He is a devoted husband and father. He is married to the love of his life, the beautiful and gifted Shannon Scott. They have six children: Kaelyn, Leah, Eden, Lawrence III, Zachary, and Reagan. Lawrence earned his Bachelor of Arts Degree in Philosophy with a minor in Business Administration from the University of Houston, a Master of Theology (ThM) Degree, and a Doctor of Ministry Degree in Leadership from Dallas Theological Seminary (DTS) in Dallas, Texas.

Willie A. Taylor is a founder and executive director of Positive Perspective Mentors and Educational Services, a non-profit 501(C)3 organization whose mission is "achieving healthier communities by mentoring, educating, and strengthening at-risk youth, individuals, and families." He serves as a Deacon at Holman Street Baptist Church, Marriage Ministry leader, and liaison for Praise, Worship, and Theatrical Arts. Willie is a songwriter, gospel artist, playwright, and director. His passion for evangelism and discipleship began in 1983 as a result of his involvement in Mission Ministry at Holman Street Baptist Church in Houston, Texas. The Singles Ministry provided a platform for the genesis of his ministry through theatrical arts. The connection of evangelism and theatrical arts was a seamless integration because of his commitment for both areas of ministry. He has been married to Dr. Michele Taylor since July 23, 1994.

Pastor Stephen Chevalier White has led From The Heart Church Ministries of Houston since July 2010. He is dedicated to perfecting the saints of God by rightly dividing the word of truth. He is committed to building families through hope, help, and healing. He founded and served as pastor of the Kingdom Builders Community Church for 10 years. Pastor White is the devoted husband of Kabrina White and father of six splendid children. Pastor White received his Master of Arts in Organizational Management from the University of Phoenix. He also served as the Division Manager of Human Resources at the Houston Airport System and a teacher and district advisory board member in the Houston Independent School District.

Pastor Herron Wilson has served as the pastor of Stranger's Home and Pilgrim Rest Baptists Churches of Shaw, Mississippi, since 1992. He's the Executive Director of Delta Missions Ministry, Inc. in Indianola, Mississippi, a faith-based ministry outreach he co-founded in 1995. Delta Missions provides weekly

Bible study, mentoring, fellowship, and recreational activities for youth, adults, and senior citizens in and around the Indianola area. Rev. Wilson received his Master of Divinity Degree from Reformed Theological Seminary in Clinton, Mississippi. Pastor Wilson was awarded the Morris Lewis Citizen of the Year Award by Indianola's Chamber of Commerce for his unswerving dedication, commitment, and achievements in local ministry. He is a pastor, Bible teacher, motivational speaker, and even once served as a co-anchor on the nightly news at a Mississippi Delta television station. He has since changed channels and networks and says his greatest joy is broadcasting the Good News of Jesus Christ and nurturing people in their walk with Christ.

ABOUT THE AUTHORS

Matthew A. Davis has served as the Pastor of New Beginning Church in Houston, Texas, since September 7, 2004. He earned his Doctorate of Transformational Leadership from Bakke Graduate University. Pastor Davis is an adjunct professor at Bakke Graduate University and Oikodome Bible Institute. As an avenue to reach the world for Jesus the Christ, *Sharing the Gospel* (2001), the workbook written by Pastor Davis, has been presented in several translations: Czech, English, Luhya, Portuguese, Spanish, Swahili, French, and Hindi. He and his wife have served as missionaries to Brazil and the Czech Republic. Pastor Davis is the father of two daughters, Megan and Macey. He proudly shares the ministries' responsibilities with his wife, Carolyn, whose musical gifts keep the youth and music ministries afloat.

Marchelle D. Lee has served in ministry since 1989. She was born in Cleveland, Ohio, and she has lived in Houston, Texas, and presently lives in San Antonio, Texas. She attends Community Bible Church under the leadership of Senior Pastor Ed Newton. Her evangelistic call has privileged her to minister in over 30-plus states in the United States, winning hundreds of souls to Jesus Christ. Marchelle has a Doctorate Degree in Theology from the Lord's Outreach School of Theology and an Associate Degree in Nursing. In her bio-vocational status, she has served as a Registered Nurse for more than 30 years. She sees nursing as a ministry and has witnessed the hand of God turn around the lives of many people. Marchelle knows firsthand how important it is to minister to people wherever needed.

Currently, she is a life coach and an Adolescent Psychiatric Nurse and enjoys ministering to the children she encounters daily. Additionally, her weekly MDL Ministries TV show ministers the Gospel of Jesus Christ in Canada, Colombia, the United Kingdom, Panama, Ireland, Costa Rica, Peru, France, the United States, Guatemala, El Salvador, Chile, Brazil, Nicaragua, and Mexico. The ministry airs on Facebook, YouTube, Roku, Amazon, and www.mdlinistries.org. She is the mother of two wonderful sons, Jeramie (Rachel) and Kenton (Jessica), grandmother of eight, and great-grandmother of five. Marchelle gives God all the glory for things He has done.

CPSIA information can be obtained
at www.ICGtesting.com
Printed in the USA
JSHW041522230423
40620JS00006B/14